Fix Your Eyes on Jesus

Running the Race Marked Out for You!

Kirkie Morrissey

For Her. For God. For Real.
faithfulwoman.com

Faithful Woman is an imprint of
Cook Communications Ministries, Colorado Springs, Colorado 80918
Cook Communications, Paris, Ontario
Kingsway Communications, Eastbourne, England

FIX YOUR EYES ON JESUS
© 2001 by Kirkie Morrissey

First Printing, 2001
Printed in the United States of America

1 2 3 4 5 6 7 8 9 10 Printing/Year 05 04 03 02 01

Editors: Wendy Peterson; Julie Smith and Craig Bubeck, Sr. Editors
Cover Design: Matthew Doherty Design
Interior Design: Matthew Doherty Design

CONTENTS

Acknowledgments 4
Introduction 6
1 Choosing Your Race 9
2 Discerning God's Races 21
3 God's Equipping for Our Races 33
4 Going for the Gold 47
5 Throwing Off All That Hinders 61
6 Forsaking the Sin That Entangles 73
7 Training for the Race 85
8 Running in Christ 97
9 Persevering When the Race Gets Tough
    Part One: Understanding God's Purposes 107
10 Persevering When the Race Gets Tough
    Part Two: Discovering *How* to Persevere 117
11 Fixing Our Eyes on Jesus .129
12 Crossing the Finish Line! .137

Endnotes 151

A Personal Note From the Author 154

❧ACKNOWLEDGMENTS❧

First and foremost, I would like to acknowledge and express my sincere gratitude to Jan Webb. This study is dedicated to her in appreciation of her passing the baton to me in this relay race of faith. While Jan was attending Wheaton College, she was one of my Young Life leaders when I was a senior at Glenbard High School, and she has remained a special friend over the years. What initially impacted me was Jan's fun spirit. I loved seeing that Christians could laugh—and Jan was hysterically funny! She also had a great attitude toward the physical challenges she experienced from having had polio as a child. That really impressed me. Yet what drew me to Christ most was Jan's caring about me. As a high schooler, to have a sharp college woman reach out to me meant a lot. We spent hours together over hamburgers, just talking. Then, as she shared the truth that Jesus loved me, I listened. Jan, along with her colaborer Ellie Swenson, opened the Scriptures to me in Campaigners, a weekly Bible study group. When Christ's invitation to know Him as my personal Savior became clear to me, I responded! Thank you, Jan. I am eternally grateful. And thank you, Ellie, and Young Life.

In addition, I would like to express my appreciation to Julie Smith, my editor at Chariot Victor. I deeply appreciate her support in processing this manuscript. I'm grateful not only for her partnership in this publishing ministry but also for her friendship. Thank you, Julie. I also thank Wendy Peterson for her hard work in the "hands-on" editing of the lengthy chapters first submitted.

One of God's most gracious gifts has been my daughter-in-law Patti, who helps me administratively and also prays for me through this process. She is a treasure. What a wonderful gift! How very special it is being family and working together. Thank you, Patti. My friend Ann also deserves my heartfelt thanks, because she reviews these studies prior to my using them with my class. Her faithful prayer support is greatly appreciated as well. Thank you, Ann.

And thank you, dear friends in Women ALIVE! Your encouragement, input, and support as we have worked through these studies together has meant so very much to me. I thank the Lord for each of you as well.

And most of all, thank You, Lord! Thank You for reaching out to me in Your love, for saving me in Your grace, drawing me deeper into Yourself in faithfulness, for calling me to ministry in Your compassion, and for enabling and empowering me by Your Spirit. *May You be glorified!* I love You, Lord Jesus.

❧ INTRODUCTION ❧

How do you view your life? Are you on the myopic end—unable to see the forest for the bark on one tree? Or do you have a more panoramic view—taking in the big picture with a sweeping perspective? Many live today with limited sight. In their lives, they are the central character. Their lives revolve around their choices and their own days.

Scripture, however, offers us a different view, a broader perspective filled with clear purpose and meaning. It unveils the truth that *we are a part of a bigger picture!* At the beginning of time, God initiated a plan that He is still carrying out today—and you and I are called to be part of it! The Hebrews 12:1-3 passage on which this study is based springboards off of Hebrews 11, chronicling many who have participated in this grand plan before us. Then we read "Therefore," which begins Hebrews 12, and it continues, "since we are surrounded by such a great cloud of witnesses, let us . . . run with perseverance the race marked out for us." From Abraham, the father of our faith, to present times, we stand in the same stream of faith as those who have gone before us. We are now surrounded by this "great cloud of witnesses" as we run our race today. (See the author's study *A Great Cloud of Witnesses* for an in-depth exploration of noted women who stand in this stream.)

A relay race is the picture that comes to mind. God called Abraham to this race and handed him the first baton. Abraham ran well and passed the baton to Isaac, who in turn passed it to Jacob. Those of faith who have already run their races before us now comprise the spectators who are cheering us on. The baton is still being passed from one generation to another.

Do you remember watching relay races at high school track meets? Do you recall the tension when your team member was making the pass to the next runner? If the baton was dropped, the crowd groaned in unison, so disappointed. But when a successful pass was made, the crowd cheered and encouraged that runner to do his or her best in that leg of the race. This picture gives us a glimpse of what is going on in the heavenlies today. As we pass the baton to others, those who have gone before watch in anticipation. If someone drops the baton—or even drops out of the race—there is sorrow and disappointment. But when we grab that baton with assurance and run with strength and conviction, there is great cheering! Elation fills the heavens! Isn't this a great picture for each of us?

This is the biblical view of life. How wonderful to be called to such a race and to participate in a story that is bigger than "just us."

The Bible reveals the bigger picture—the true story for our lives. Our lives *do* have purpose and meaning. Each of us is called to participate. The race we are called to, however, is different from the races run in this world. We are not competing with one another. We are not driven in this race. God orders our steps and seasons—and we move in Him, with Him, and for Him. It's a freeing race—an exciting one.

The key to running this race—the key to life itself—is clearly stated: "Fix your eyes on Jesus." He is not only our encouragement to persevere when the going gets rough, but He is our motivation in running. He is our goal—our gold!

There is a baton being handed to you and to me. All who have gone before are cheering us on. You and I are called to "fix our eyes on Jesus" and "run with perseverance the race marked out for us." Is your heart pounding as you hear this call? Mine is! This study explores the reality of this race and how we can run it well.

On your mark. . . . Get set. . . . *go!*

Therefore, since we are surrounded by such a great cloud of witnesses, let us throw off everything that hinders and the sin that so easily entangles, and let us run with perseverance the race marked out for us. Let us fix our eyes on Jesus, the author and perfecter of our faith, who for the joy set before him endured the cross, scorning its shame, and sat down at the right hand of the throne of God. Consider him who endured such opposition from sinful men, so that you will not grow weary and lose heart.

(Heb. 12:1-3)

Choosing Your Race

Life offers so many options! All that the world holds out to us can potentially be ours. How thrilling and challenging! The appeal of all we see, the urging from others, and our own drive to excel and achieve can motivate us to jump into many races being run in the world. We're encouraged to make our mark and gain self-worth through achievement and accumulation of things. In fact, one of the most popular television shows today is "Who Wants to Be a Millionaire." As entertaining as this show is, it reveals a deeper sign of our times. This race for more money to buy more things has become so strong that the time in which we're living has become known as the era of greed.

"The rat race" is one humorous (though telling) term frequently used to describe these races of life. Those participating, however, often experience incredible stress, which can take its toll on health and family. Are these races worth the effort and sacrifice? Is this what life is about?

In the challenge to "go for the gold" in life, many prizes are offered as the gold. Advertisers portray their products, such as cars and houses, as the gold to possess. The corporate structure holds up position as the gold, encouraging employees to climb higher and faster up the ladder of success. For athletes, winning the Super Bowl or an Olympic medal qualifies as the gold.

What does the Bible say? Throughout Scripture, the metaphor of a race is also used to refer to life. As our key passage for this study,

Hebrews 12:1-3, clearly states, *there is a race marked out for each of us*. The Apostle Paul also refers to this race of life: "I consider my life worth nothing to me, if only I may finish the race and complete the task the Lord Jesus has given me—the task of testifying to the gospel of God's grace" (Acts 20:24). Then at the conclusion of Paul's life, he proclaims his success in 2 Timothy 4:7 stating, "I have fought the good fight, I have finished the race, I have kept the faith."

Paul may have picked up his imagery from the Olympian Games, which were very popular in his day, and the race, in particular, was an important sport. Because of the popularity of these games, the metaphor of a race to describe life may have been fresh in Paul's mind. However, rather than the "gold" of the Olympic Games being our goal, we run with our eyes fixed on a prize of much greater worth: Christ Himself!

In addition to the race and the gold, the Olympics had a tradition of lighting a torch in Olympia, Greece, several weeks prior to the opening. A runner took this flaming torch and began his journey across the country. Once the torch arrived there, a series of runners carried it in relays to the Olympic site, the temple of Zeus. It was considered a great honor—as it still is today—to be one of these relay runners carrying the torch. Those runners were called "heralds of peace."

This symbol of the Olympic torch is a powerful one for our relay of faith. Think of Pentecost, the day Christ's church actually began, when tongues of fire came down from heaven and rested on each of the disciples. This fulfilled Jesus' promise and commission to them before He returned to heaven: "You will receive power when the Holy Spirit comes on you; and you will be my witnesses . . . to the ends of the earth" (Acts 1:8). At that moment, a new heat in the relay began, and the disciples became true "heralds of peace"—proclaiming true peace from God, with God, and of God. This torch has passed from generation to generation and its light has spread throughout the earth—and each of us is invited to have the honor of being a "torch bearer." This is an exciting race to be a part of, and the gold has eternal value!

The contrast between the world's races and God's race brings before us a choice: Which race will we run? What gold will we strive for? To consider our options and reflect on our choices, let's turn to God's Word.

Biblical Discovery and Reflection

1. What races does the world set before us? What are the appeals of each?

2. Is it true that there is a *specific race*, unique to each of us, which God calls us to? What is clearly stated in Ephesians 2:10?

3. How is this truth illustrated in Jeremiah 1:4-5, Acts 22:10, and 1 Corinthians 3:5?

4. In considering God's plan, what do we discover about the Lord's ways for us in Isaiah 48:17-18?

5. What qualities of His plans can we discern from Jeremiah 29:11 and John 10:10?

6. Listed below are Scriptures revealing your *true identity* (and consequently, your worth). Personalize these truths as you read them.

   a. Who created you according to Psalm 100:3, 139:13-16; Isaiah 44:24, and 46:3-4?

   b. Who are you, according to the following verses?
      Deuteronomy 26:18
      2 Corinthians 6:18; 1 John 3:1
      Romans 8:16-17; Galatians 4:6-7

7. What is God's heart for you, as clearly stated in 1 John 3:1 above (see also 1 John 4:10)?

8. Henri Nouwen summarizes these truths in his book *Life of the Beloved*. He writes:

   Long before any person spoke to us in this world, we are spoken to by the voice of eternal love. Our precious-ness, uniqueness and individuality are not given to us by those who meet us in clock-time—our brief chronological existence—but by the One who has chosen us with an everlasting love, a love that existed from all eternity and will last through all eternity.
   . . . We are the Beloved. We are intimately loved long before our parents, teachers, spouses, children and friends loved or wounded us. That's the truth of our lives. . . .
   That's the truth spoken by the voice that says, "You are my Beloved."
   Listening to that voice with great inner attentiveness, I hear at my center words that say: "I have called you by

name, from the very beginning. You are mine and I am yours. You are my Beloved. . . . I have molded you in the depths of the earth and knitted you together in your mother's womb. I have carved you in the palms of my hands and hidden you in the shadow of my embrace."[2]

What is your response to these biblical truths, as expressed by Nouwen as well as explored in the Scriptures so far?

9. Why is it important to know who you are when it comes to choosing the race you are going to run?

Personal Application and Response

10. Eugene Peterson, in *Run with the Horses*, summarizes the preceding views:

> Our lives are not puzzles to be figured out. Rather, we come to God, who knows us and reveals to us the truth of our lives. . . .
>
> . . . If we are going to live appropriately, we must be aware that we are living in the middle of a story that was begun and will be concluded by another. And this other is God.
>
> . . . How much better it is if we take the time to get the drift of things, to find out where we fit. The story into which life fits is already well on its way when we walk into the room.[3]

Are these views new to you? What perspective do these truths give you about your life?

11. The hurts—those wounds—we receive in life can deceive us into believing that we're not special and that there isn't a race we are called to. Have you struggled with such feelings? Will you not only give intellectual assent to these wonderful truths of who you are but also accept them in your heart? If so, what practical things can you do to help establish yourself in them?

12. In *Calm My Anxious Heart*, Linda Dillow reflects:

> [When David asserted that his times were in God's hands (Ps. 31:15)], it means that the Almighty Creator of the universe prepared a purpose for us to walk in. God acted with definite purpose when He created you because He had a plan for you to fulfill. How loved and unique you are! All of your abilities—and your disabilities—were created to fit the unique plan God has for you. No one can fulfill your purpose but you. And God's plan for you and His plan for me embrace far more than the events or circumstances that happen to us. They also embrace what God wants us to be and do and what He desires to do in and through us.[4]

a. As you discover the truths regarding who you are and God's call on your life, what fears, if any, surface with your discoveries? Explain.

b. What questions do your discoveries raise?

c. What excitement do these truths create within you? Be specific.

13. Although God created us and has specific plans for us, He gave us our freedom of choice—out of His love for us, He did not want to force His plans on us. What choice did some of the Israelites make, according to Jeremiah 6:16-17? How do you see people making this choice today?

14. Some of these truths for us are symbolically and dramatically portrayed in the children's movie *The Lion King.* Simba, a lion cub, was a child of royalty, born to Mufasa, the king of the pride in Africa's Serengeti. Wanting to be king himself, Simba's Uncle Scar deviously arranged the death of Mufasa, making it appear that Simba had been responsible. Terrified, Simba ran away. Through a series of events, he encountered a warthog named Pumbaa and his fun friend Timon, a meerkat. They introduced him to their lifestyle of "Hakuna Matata"—a philosophy of "no worries," in which they lived solely for themselves and for pleasure. Soon Simba forgot his royal identity and adopted their carefree lifestyle over his regal responsibilities. However, one day, years later, his childhood companion Nala found him as she was desperately looking for help for her people. Under Scar's evil reign, the land had become desecrated. There was no longer vegetation or food to sustain life. The animals were oppressed, and the need was great. Nala pleaded with him to help. Simba was torn within. The appeal of continuing his present lifestyle of pleasure was tempting. To think of returning and getting involved created many fears within. How would he be received? What dangers would he face? The personal risk was great. Yet, in the end, he responded to the call to be more and to make a difference. Simba returned to fulfill his destiny.

    What parallels do you see between your life and the biblical story of what has happened in our world? In what ways, if any, can you identify with Simba's feelings as he became aware of the call on his life?

15. Examine the choices that pull you—what races appeal to you? What is involved in running each? What do you think the rewards are of each? The issue here is not what is in our life but what has captured our heart. See the chart below.

What race?	What's involved?	What rewards?

16. At the end of your life, what do you think will matter the most? A popular bumper sticker reads: "He who dies with the most toys wins." What are your thoughts?

17. If you were to summarize what your life is about in a word or a phrase, what would it be? Is this what you want it to be?

18. My friend "Barbara's" mother was upset when Barbara chose to give her life to Christ when she was in high school. Her family ridiculed her beliefs and openly rejected her and the Lord. Late in life, her mother was diagnosed with cancer. When she was close to death, a friend of hers died. Mustering strength, she attended her friend's memorial service. Her friend had been a Christian and her life had impacted many. As Barbara's mom listened to the eulogies, her own life flashed before her. What a

contrast she saw. She could just imagine what would be said about her at her funeral. Later that week, while watching television from her bed, she was flipping through channels and came across Billy Graham preaching at a crusade. Instead of cursing, as she had in the past, she listened. When a phone number flashed on the screen to talk with a counselor, she picked up the phone. Responding to her questions kindly, this counselor called her back the next day . . . and the next—until Barbara's mother came to an understanding of who Jesus is and how He had died for her. She then opened her heart to the Lord Jesus Christ as her Savior. Her life immediately and dramatically changed! Everyone could see the difference in her. She grieved over how she had lived and what she had done. Calling each family member to her bedside, she asked for forgiveness. The Spirit turned her cursing to blessing! She radiated joy in the Lord, and spoke freely of Him to all. She left this world in peace and entered God's heavenly kingdom with joy.

a. Because we have only one life to live, how important it is to make a conscious choice regarding what our life will be about and how we will live it! How sad to reach the end of our life and be filled with regrets. What choices have you made about how you will live your life?

b. At any point, we can choose differently—just as "Barbara's" mom did. In some ways, God's plans are like those moving sidewalks that run through airports. We can choose to step on at any point and get right in the stream of things headed toward the goal. This is what the Lord desires us to do. What is His invitation to you, expressed in Isaiah 55:1-3?

19. Ken Gire, in *Windows of the Soul,* reflects on the symbolism in Tolkien's *The Hobbit.* The magician Gandalf told Bilbo Baggins, "There is more to you than you know." Gire writes,

> He said this, knowing that within the hobbit's veins coursed blood not only from the sedentary Baggins side of the family but also from the swashbuckling Took side. We have a similar mingling of blood within us from a lineage that is both human and divine. . . .
>
> Most of the time, though, we are burrowed away in our hobbit holes and don't give a thought to our heritage. . . . When Bilbo Listened to an ancient song . . .
>
> . . . Something Tookish woke up inside him, and he wished to go and see the great mountains, and hear the pine-trees and the waterfalls, and explore the caves, and wear a sword instead of a walking stick. . . .
>
> . . . Something "Tookish" wakes in me, a sleepy-eyed awareness that there is more to me than I know. And suddenly I want to set aside my walking stick and strap on a sword, and leave the cozy security of my hobbit hole in search of some far-off adventure.[5]

a. Has something "Tookish" awakened in you as you've explored these Scriptures? Do you have a new awareness that "there is more to you than you know"? Are you ready for God's call to an adventure—to a race—that is a part of a bigger story? What choices would you like to make now as you reflect on the truths of this lesson?

b. Express your heart to the Lord regarding your desires for your life.

20. In conclusion, meditate on the truths expressed in this study's key Scripture passage, Hebrews 12:1-3. Write out these verses in your own words, personalizing them.

🔖 Group Discussion Questions

1. What reservations, or fears, might people have in choosing to run God's race?

2. What tension can we experience as we desire to run "the race marked out for us" yet feel the pressures of the other races being run all around us, perhaps finding them appealing as well? What have you personally discovered in this? How can we stay focused on the race God calls us to and keep our eyes "fixed on Jesus"?

3. Does God intend for us not to enjoy the things of "this world" if we are running His race? What is the primary issue, do you think? Can you give an example to support your response?

4. What can happen if we don't consciously reflect on our life and the choices that are before us? Is that something you think people generally do? What has your own experience been in this? By reflecting on this in this lesson, what have you discovered?

🎕 2 🎖

Discerning God's Races

A variety of races are promoted in life, often with appealing prizes. Sometimes a prize isn't even necessary, because the races themselves are for such good causes. All types of organizations recruit participants for their programs, and other individuals request help with their needs. How can we *know* which of these races really serves God?

And what about *time?* We may already feel overwhelmed with all we have to do. How do we fit in another race, even if it is God's? Responsibilities, like family and career, place daily demands on us—are we supposed to wait until after children leave home or until we retire to have time for God's races? Or are the priorities in our lives now part of God's race, with the specific tasks the Lord has prepared integrated around these? Are the various "heats" in our race all ordered?

Because the Lord has designed our individual marathon of life with eternal significance, it is of utmost importance to Him for us to know these details! In addition, since He created us, loves us, and designed the races specifically for us, it is also in His heart to guide us in each detail. He is sovereign Lord, so He is in control of all that is a part of our lives. He is able to order our steps.

These are life-changing truths. As we experience these realities, our days have purpose and our God becomes increasingly exciting. Consequently, not only does our joy in Him deepen, but we exclaim, as did Eric Liddell in *Chariots of Fire*: "When I run, I feel His pleasure!" What an adventure awaits us!

Biblical Discovery and Reflection

1. Jesus is a wonderful example of One who knew the race set out for Him. He came with specific purposes of eternal significance, loved all He met, and was besieged daily by their needs and demands. Yet He walked in peace, with a clear sense of His Father's purpose and direction.

    a. To explore this, record your discoveries from the passages below.

Reference	Pressures or Demands	How Jesus Responded
Luke 4:40-44		
Luke 5:12-16		

    b. What strikes you personally from these examples?

    c. How do the stresses of Jesus' life compare with yours? Be specific. What does His example communicate regarding the demands on you?

    d. What was Jesus' secret, revealed in Luke 4:42 and 5:16?

    e. Did Jesus have extra time on His hands? What do you learn from His example?

2. Jesus knew His priorities and was clear about what the Father had for Him to do when faced with various demands. How are these truths illustrated in Luke 4:42-43 above? See also John 11, specifically verses 1-6, 14, and 38-44.

3. Because Jesus was God incarnate, was knowing what the Father had for Him to do unique to Him? Can this be our experience as well? What insight do you gain from the Apostle Paul's claim in Acts 23:1?

4. What are we bid in Galatians 5:25?

   a. Could ours be a step-by-step walk each day, just as Jesus' was? Could God guide us as He did Paul, so we, too, could be assured that we had done all that God had for us to do? See Proverbs 20:24 and Ephesians 2:10.

   b. What is your initial response to this possibility?

5. In order to enter the race and walk—or run—in the Spirit, there is an essential "first step."

   a. Identify what is necessary from the following verses: John 3:5-7, 16; Revelation 3:20.

   b. Have you taken this first step? If not, would you like to do so? Express your heart to the Lord here. What is His promise to you in Revelation 3:20?

6. With Christ living in us, what occurs in our lives, according to Romans 8:9a, 14?

7. What does the Apostle Paul exhort us to do in Romans 12:1-2, and what does he say will result?

8. Read Romans 12:1-2 more closely, and distinguish between what is our responsibility and what is the Lord's.

9. As we yield to Him and ask Him to lead us daily, what will He do, expressed by Jesus in John 10:3-4 (see also Ps. 23:3b; 32:8)?

10. Two means through which the Lord guides are considered below.

    a. What major tool does God use, according to Psalm 119:105, 130?

    b. What is another means of guidance, from Colossians 1:9 and James 1:5?

    c. Can you give an example of how the Lord has led you through either of these means?

11. Another major way in which the Lord guides our steps as we go through our day is by the freedom and the restraint of His Spirit.

a. How are these two ways illustrated in Acts 8:29 and 16:6-8?

b. Too often, believers give the Lord their lives, then take back their days! But the Lord desires to direct our steps on a daily basis. A major way He does this is through the freedom and restraint of His Spirit, illustrated above. As we stay close to Him, we become increasingly sensitive to His Spirit within us and in so doing keep in step with His Spirit.

    (1) We have three responsibilities: First, to abide in Him, spending time with Him each day. Second, to yield our agendas to Him, asking Him to lead us through the day. And third, to remain sensitive to His Spirit within and obey as He leads. Before committing to anything (an appointment, a lunch, etc.), ask the Lord to guide—then pay attention to His freedom or restraint regarding both if and when you should do it.

    (2) His responsibilities are to guide us and to fulfill His purposes as we go, which He *promises* to do. Not only does He lead in the plans He has, but He also beautifully orders our steps in the priorities and responsibilities of our life.

c. Jesus walked with this sensitivity to God's Spirit. An example of this would be His "detour" into Samaria, where the Father wanted Him to meet a woman who needed to know His love (John 4:1-26.) Another time, Jesus zeroed in on Zacchaeus from among the crowds and said, "I must stay at your house today" (Luke 19:1-10). If we remain sensitive to His Spirit, He will lead us in the same ways today. For example, have you ever gone to the phone to make a call and found yourself restrained from lifting the receiver? Or at times have you felt compelled to make a call, write someone a note, invite a couple over for dinner, or meet a friend for lunch? This can be the Spirit acting within you, guiding you. Can you give an example from your own life?

d. An example from my experience of paying attention to God's ordering is when a friend needed people to stay with her throughout the day when she returned home following surgery for a brain tumor. My heart's desire was to help, and an available time slot came up on Wednesday from 12:00-5:00. As I quickly prayed about this before committing, I sensed restraint from agreeing to the entire time but had freedom to commit to 3:00-5:00, which I did. It worked out that the person who agreed to be there from 12:00-3:00 had a great need herself. When I arrived at 3:00, my friend was sleeping so this other person and I had a special time together. Both of us were aware that God had ordered our steps.

     A frequent experience of mine involves when I go to the grocery store. As I seek God's timing, it has been thrilling to me to see how the Lord arranges divine encounters there. (Just as He met the woman at the well!)

     The truth of how the Lord orders our steps has been one of the most life-changing discoveries for me! As I entrust all to Him, it thrills me to see Him put everything in its proper order—my priorities, responsibilities, needs, and His purposes! He also gives needed discernment when a request comes to spend time with someone, whether that's for me to do or not, and if so, when. Seeing Him so intricately involved in every detail of my life heightens my joy in Him and deepens my awe of Him. As He does so, I have the sense that I am fulfilling the purposes He has for me. It's exciting for me, and I pray that I am glorifying Him.

e. Frank Laubach endorsed these truths when he wrote of his experience as a missionary in the Philippines: "This sense of cooperation with God in little things is what so astonishes me, for I never have felt it this way before. . . . My part is to live this hour in continuous inner conversation with God and in perfect responsiveness to his will."[1]

f. Are these truths new to you? What is your response to the reality that the Lord desires to order *your* steps each day? This experience is something that will grow over time, as we increasingly yield our agendas to Him throughout the day and maintain a continuing dialogue with Him. Often, we may not be aware of what He does through us—and many times He guides simply as our Good Shepherd, taking care of us in our needs.

12. Philippians 2:13 talks about God working in these ways. What does it proclaim?

a. Hannah Whitall Smith writes: "Having surrendered [the soul's] will into the keeping of the Lord, He works in it to will and to do His good pleasure, and the soul finds itself really *wanting* to do the things God wants it to do."[2]

b. Can you give an example of how you have experienced this reality?

13. A further way in which the Lord works within us is by giving us a burden and then leading us in it, going before us to fulfill His purposes. This is often a way He works for those involvements He has for "a time and season."

a. An example of this is seen in how the Lord directed Nehemiah in the task He had for him, recorded in Nehemiah 1:3-4; 2:1-6, 17. What do you discover?

b. Watchman Nee reaffirms this when he writes, "We must seek to do His will in everything and wait on Him in His work until He communicates His burden to us. His burden is the manifestation of His will. The burden we receive is the very will of God, and it is also the means by which God manifests His will."[3]

c. One example from my own life of this was in the 1980s, when my husband and I learned of the needs of the boat people escaping from Vietnam. As we saw photos from refugee camps in Malaysia, our hearts went out to these dear people, and we became burdened to help. We wanted to have a family stay with us for awhile in the "mother-in-law apartment" we had in the lower level of our home.

   Not knowing how to go about sponsoring a family, we asked the Lord that if He truly wanted a family to stay with us, that He would lead us to the appropriate contact. The very next day in our newspaper, the headline of our Metro section read: "Homes Needed for Refugee Families"! In that article was the name of the woman we needed to contact, along with her phone number!

   Within a few months, a precious family arrived—a husband and wife with their two-year-old daughter and six-month-old son and the husband's brother. This turned out to be a wonderful experience for our family, and everyone in that Vietnamese family came to know the Lord.

14. As we seek God's direction and guidance, the accompanying inner peace we receive is a confirmation that we are being obedient to what God is asking. The Lord, then, uses rest and unrest as a means of guiding us. Can you give an example of when you have experienced this?

Personal Application and Response

15. What are your initial thoughts as you meditate on your discoveries above? What feelings are you experiencing?

16. Jesus said to His Father, "Here I am. . . . I have come to do your will, O God" (Heb. 10:7). Is this your heart as well? How would you complete the sentence: "Here I am . . . I have come to do_____"?

17. Do you hesitate to let go of your agenda—either for your life or for your day? If so, what is underlying this hesitancy? Process this with the Lord. Bring Him your fears, your hopes, and your dreams.

18. Since we are faced daily with choices of running our own race and pushing our own agendas or walking as God directs and yielding to His purposes, what powerful truths are important to remember, according to Paul in 1 Corinthians 6:19-20 and 2 Corinthians 5:14-15?

    a. What are your reactions to these verses?

    b. Sheila Walsh's perspective is this: "The whole purpose of our lives is to glorify God, to say with every fiber of our beings that we exist for him."[4] As we choose to live not for ourselves but for Him—existing solely for Him—what do you think will be the results?

    c.   Frank Sinatra's old song "I Did It My Way" conveys the world's perspective of how life should be lived. In light of the truths in this lesson, what is your response to this claim?

19.   When we become willful, or simply "mess up," what will God do if we want a fresh start (see Lam. 3:22-23; 1 John 1:9)? Take time to confess anything to Him that is on your heart—then thank Him for His forgiveness and mercy.

20.   Now that you've seen how critical it is to fellowship with the Lord each day in His Word and in prayer, when will you schedule this time in (if you haven't already)? How will you make the time, if your days are full? Reflect on Jesus' example in question 1. Examine your days. Ask for the Lord's guidance as to what, if anything, you need to eliminate or rearrange. Schedule this time in as a commitment, as you would with a friend—then keep it as a priority.

21.   Are there specific actions God is calling you to—an area of need He wants you to be involved in, an individual He would have you reach out to, or one of your family He is guiding you to spend time with? Seek His guidance. Record anything specific on your heart at this time.

22.   As you walk through your days, remain sensitive to His Spirit. Ask for God's guidance in each step. Trust Him to order your needs, priorities, responsibilities, and the tasks He has prepared for you. Record your discoveries.

23. What will be the results of your life as you run with Him, according to John 15:5-8, 16?

24. Express your heart to God now, offering yourself to Him for His purposes, if you so desire.

Group Discussion Questions

1. What are your reactions to God's leading *you* each step of every day? Is God big enough to do this for everyone? Do you think He has more important things to do? Why would it be essential for Him to order our steps?

2. What fears might we have in entrusting ourselves and every area of our life to Him? How can these be overcome?

3. Although we may desire to keep in step with His Spirit, what problems might we have actually doing so in the midst of the demands of our day? How can we remember to yield to Him as we go? Can you give a specific example?

4. What insights in this lesson have helped you understand the importance of spending time daily with the Lord? Generally, what difficulties can we face in actually taking this time? What specific obstacles do you face? Brainstorm on how these can be overcome. Hold one another accountable, if you desire.

5. What hope do the truths of this lesson give you—for the present as well as for the future? What feelings do you have as you consider these realities?

❦ 3 ❦

God's Equipping for Our Races

Have you noticed all the special equipment and designer clothing runners have? Specialized running shoes are available as well, depending on the type of running one does and the terrain one covers. Available also are waist-packs equipped with water bottles for short runs and small day-packs with room for more food and equipment for slightly longer runs. Heart-rate monitors can be worn for health purposes, and specially designed watches not only give you the time but also your current altitude and distance covered, for example. In taking running seriously, proper equipment is important in facing the challenges that can present themselves, as well as in simply making the run more comfortable.

The Lord calls us to our individual races, but are we on our own to do the best we can? Or does He provide the "equipment" we need, especially designed for the uniqueness of who we are and the terrain in which we're running? Perhaps our race is more like a triathlon and includes other events, such as swimming and cycling. Does the Lord equip us in general, but then we need to adapt to the specific uniqueness of our races?

And what about "style"? It's easy to look at others—how they're equipped and how they run—and think that's how we are to function as well. In our races in this world, it's easy to allow how others race to affect not only what we do but how we feel about how we are doing. Is this what God has for us though? Let us turn to God's Word to see what the Lord reveals regarding how He uniquely equips and designs each of us for our specific races.

Biblical Discovery and Reflection

1. What have you noticed often influences believers in how they run their races or serve in their responsibilities? On what have you based your personal style of running?

2. David illustrates for us some important lessons regarding how we are to function as God calls us. Read 1 Samuel 17:25-51.

   a. Who was David at this time?

   b. In God's calling him to fight the giant Goliath, what could David have felt? Put yourself in his place. What thoughts might he have had regarding his own ability to fight this mighty soldier?

   c. How did King Saul attempt to equip David for this task in verses 38-39? How do people attempt to do this with others today?

   d. What did David realize, recorded in verses 39-40?

   e. Where was David's confidence as he went out to meet Goliath? See verses 45-47.

   f. What resulted?

g. What lessons are there for you in this? Be specific.

3. Having discovered that the Lord has already prepared specific plans for each of us (Eph. 2:10), what do we learn of God's equipping for these tasks in 1 Corinthians 12:4-11?

4. To whom does Paul say God gives these spiritual gifts? See verse 1 Corinthians 12:7 as well as 1 Peter 4:10. What does this mean for *you?* What is your response to this discovery?

5. These Scriptures also give another glimpse of the bigger picture we are a part of. What do you discover in 1 Corinthians 12:12-31?

    a. Why would it be critical to discover what gift or gifts you have been given?

    b. How would knowing your gift(s) help you discern what tasks the Lord might have for you? Can you give an example of how this has helped you in the past?

6. What do these truths communicate to you regarding your worth and importance?

7. Regarding the choices and responsibility we have in using our gifts, consider Jesus' Parable of the Talents in Matthew 25:14-30. (A talent in Jesus' day was a monetary designation. Today it also represents all gifts He entrusts us with.)

   a. First, to whom did the talents belong, discerned from verses 14-15? What does this communicate to you?

   b. On what basis were these talents given? How does this help free you from fear? Explain.

   c. Why do you think Jesus would give people differing amounts? How does this apply to His gifting of His body?

   d. What choices did the servant who was entrusted with one talent make?

      (1) Was his understanding of his master, who represents the Lord, accurate?

      (2) How do people today make the same mistake regarding using their gifts?

      (3) Do you have any fears regarding who the Lord is as He calls you to serve Him? If so, what are these, and how will you discover whether or not this truly is His character?

   e. What did the two faithful servants receive when the master returned? What do you notice regarding their rewards? What does this say to you?

f. What is most meaningful to you regarding your giftedness from this parable?

8. Do we merit or earn a certain gift? What do you discover in 1 Corinthians 12:11, Ephesians 4:7-8, and Hebrews 2:4.

    a. In the Ephesians passage above, the words *grace* and *gifts* are used interchangeably. We discover from the original Greek that the word for *gifts* is *charismata* and the word for *grace* is *charis*. Wonderfully, *grace* is the root of *gifts!* What does this mean to you personally?

    b. Additional insight into the nature of these gifts is gained from the words used to describe them in 1 Corinthians 12:7. How are they defined here?

        (1) One of the Greek words for "gifts" is *pneumatika*, meaning "things belonging to the Spirit"—not our possession. How does this relate to the Parable of the Talents?

        (2) What does this say about us taking pride in the gifts we are given?

Personal Application and Response

9. Some of the truths explored thus far regarding the importance of discovering our gifts are: each of us has been given at least one gift; these gifts help guide in discerning God's purposes for our lives; and they are essential in the effective functioning of His body in this world. In light of these, take time now to explore what gift or gifts God has lovingly given you. It is His heart's desire that you know what these are! So, as you begin exploring the avenues of discovery below, ask the Lord to give you insight and open your eyes to His equipping.

   a. Carefully and prayerfully read the "gift passages" of Romans 12:4-8; 1 Corinthians 12:4-11, 28; Ephesians 4:11; and 1 Peter 4:7-11. Reflect on the definitions of these gifts provided in the list following this chapter. On this list, underline the one(s) you think you may have been given.

   b. As you reflected on the gifts identified, were there any you hoped you had been given? Draw a heart next to those on the gift list. The Lord often puts in our hearts a desire to do what He's called us to do.

   c. For further insight, consider the tasks you have previously undertaken, filling in the chart below.

Tasks Performed	Gifts Needed	Results Experienced or Affirmation Received

Considering your discoveries above, what gift(s) do you think you have been given? Put a check by these on the list. (Put a question mark beside any you aren't sure about but think may be a possibility.)

d. Reflecting on the chart above, what tasks energized you? Which ones drained you? When we're functioning in our gifts, we usually feel energized from the task, even though we can be physically tired. Functioning outside of our gifts generally leaves us drained. Put a star by these "energizers" on your list.

e. What are your areas of interest, and what burdens are on your heart? What need excites you if you were to become involved in it? Put a smiley face by the gift(s) needed.

f. Another indication of how you are gifted is how you respond when a need arises. When a family has a crisis, what do you do? Do you offer to help clean before other family arrives? Do you bring food? Do you organize volunteers to provide meals? Do you open your home to those who come from out of town? Do you give money to help with financial needs? Do you go be with the family to provide comfort, support, and encouragement? On the list, mark the gift(s) involved in how you respond with a cross.

g. Ask three people who know you well and who have seen you at work what gift(s) they think you have been given. Others can see in us things that are more difficult to see in ourselves. Mark these gifts with a number sign (#).

h. As you review your discoveries above, what are your conclusions regarding the gift(s) you've been given? Record
these below. Ask the Lord to confirm what He has given to
you.

10. Reflect on what you've discovered so far.

a. What are your responses to the realization that God has
given you a spiritual gift, or gifts, identified above?

b. What fears, if any, do you have? Come to the Lord with
each. What truths regarding who He is help free you from
these fears? Be specific.

c. What hopes do you now have for your life? Express your
heart to the Lord in these.

11. When you are asked to help with a project or take on a task,
what will you now do in evaluating whether you will accept? Be
specific.

12. Elizabeth O'Connor, in *Eighth Day of Creation*, has some helpful
insights and words of encouragement concerning functioning in
our gift(s).

a. She writes: "When I become aware of my own gifts and give
my attention to communicating what is in me . . . I have the
experience of growing toward wholeness. I am working out
God's 'chosen purpose,' and I am no longer dependent on

what others think and how they respond. . . . I am content to be nobody because I know that in the important inner realm of the Spirit I am somebody." She goes on to say that "when God calls a person he calls him into the fulness of his own potential."[1]

b. Regarding feelings of competition or jealousy toward others and their gifts, she says:

Helpful in dealing with our envy or jealousy is the knowledge that these feelings are giving us clear warning that we have abandoned ourselves. If we keep our attention focused on the other person, we only increase our pain and anxiety. Envy is a symptom of lack of appreciation of our own uniqueness and self-worth. Each of us has something to give that no one else has to give. . . .

. . . One of the certain signs that we are at the periphery of our lives is our beginning to wonder whether or not what we are doing will be pleasing to others. Whenever we begin to act and produce with the approval of others in mind, there comes the haunting possibility that we will not live up to their actual or imagined expectations. To the degree that this feeling takes over we abandon ourselves, and spontaneity and creativity die in us. We enter into the sin of judging our own works, of deciding what is good and what is bad, when our only task is to be faithful over what we have—to do the best we can with it and to leave the judgment to God. We do not have to be better than others, or live up to their expectations, or fulfill their demands.[2]

c. How are her words encouraging to you?

d. Why is where we fix our eyes critical? What have you personally discovered regarding this?

13. As you reflect on this lesson, summarize your discoveries below.
Who you are:
Your worth:
Your gifts:

14. Review the responses of the stewards in the Parable of the Talents (question 7). Which one can you identify with? What will you do now in response to your discoveries?

15. What do the truths of this lesson communicate to you regarding having to push for your place in life?

16. How do your discoveries set you free? Explain.

17. What can the impact of your life be? What are your responses to this realization?

18. In conclusion, personalize Paul's prayer in Colossians 1:9-13.

Group Discussion Questions

1. Do you have difficulty accepting that some people are given more gifts than others? Why or why not? Do the number of gifts indicate one's value to God? Explain and give examples.

2. Are those with the more visible gifts more important? Is serving quietly significant? How do the world's values influence our perspectives?

3. What choices are we faced with in the discovering of our gifts? What, if any, do you struggle with?

4. What do people miss by not realizing their spiritual giftedness and their place in God's kingdom? What responsibility do we have in communicating the truth that there is more to life than what is generally offered by the world?

5. Having completed this lesson, what gift(s) does it appear you may have been given? Ask those in your group for their insights into your giftedness. Share with them your feelings regarding your discoveries.

6. What perspective do the truths of this lesson give to the value of your life? How can we maintain an eternal perspective as we go throughout our days? What pressures have the potential of drawing us back into the values of the world? How can these be overcome?

7. What were the most exciting discoveries of this lesson for you? How will they change your life? Be specific.

Definitions of Spiritual Gifts

Administration: The Spirit-given ability to organize and administrate details and business needs.

Apostleship: The Spirit-given desire to go to previously unchurched areas to communicate the Gospel and establish churches.

Compassion: The Spirit-given ability to respond to hurting individuals with sensitive understanding and genuine empathy.

Discernment of spirits: Two aspects: (1) the Spirit-given ability to distinguish between persons or the works of God and those of Satan; and (2) Spirit-given insight of un-Christlike spirits in a Christian (such as the spirit of jealousy).

Encouragement: The Spirit-given ability to act or speak to upbuild, strengthen, and uplift others.

Evangelism: A burden for people to know Christ as Savior, along with the Spirit-given ability to proclaim the salvation message in Christ with clarity and conviction.

Exhortation: The Spirit-given ability to see an area in which an individual needs correction and encouragement and to help that person in an effective way.

Faith: The Spirit-given ability to know what the Lord desires to do in a situation and to confidently believe He will accomplish it.

Giving: The desire to give money and material possessions to others with sensitivity to the leading of the Spirit in doing so effectively.

Healing: The Spirit-given ability to dispense the Lord's power to accomplish the healing of individual needs—mentally, emotionally, spiritually, and/or physically.

Hospitality: The Spirit-given ability to warmly and graciously share one's home with others.

Knowledge: Two aspects: (1) The Spirit-given awareness of facts about a person, situation, or our world (for example, Jesus with the Samaritan woman in John 4); and (2) the ability to understand, retain, and apply facts and truths about God and His Word.

Leadership: The Spirit-given ability to govern and lead others with vision, purpose, and direction.

Mercy: The Spirit-given ability to reach out to the unlovely and hurting of this world, bringing love and aid to them.

Miracles: The outworking of the Spirit through an individual to accomplish a variety of supernatural acts.

Pastor: The Spirit-given ability to love, care for, guide, and nurture a specific group of Christians.

Preaching: The Spirit-given ability to present the Gospel clearly and compellingly. (Focus is primarily on "what"—what we're to do or be and what God has for us.)

Prophecy: Two aspects: (1) the Spirit's revelation to a person of what is to come; and (2) the ability to clarify Scripture for the sake of action.

Serving: The Spirit-given desire, insight, will, and skill to help others in practical, tangible ways, bringing aid, strength, and encouragement to them.

Teaching: The Spirit-given ability to understand God's Word and to communicate it effectively to others for application. (Focus is developing the "what" with "how" and "why.")

Tongues: Two aspects: (1) the Spirit-given ability to speak another language without learning it; and (2) a Spirit-inspired "prayer language" of unknown utterance.

Interpretation of tongues: Two aspects: (1) the Spirit-given ability to understand what someone is saying in another language without learning it; and (2) the Spirit-given ability to understand and make known to others what another believer has spoken in a "prayer tongue."

Wisdom: The Spirit-given ability to give wise counsel and to act and speak in a discerning, insightful manner.

❧ 4 ❧

Going for the Gold

Olympic athletes train with one goal in mind: Winning a gold medal for their country. This is the focus of their lives for years. Because of how much they value the prize, they don't count the cost. They accept personal sacrifice willingly, giving their all toward their goal.

According to Hebrews 12, each of us is called to a specific race. What does it mean for us to go for the gold? What are the goals God has set before us in the race He calls us to? Are we willing to give this race our all, as athletes do for a tangible gold medal—or will we give it less? As we reflect on this, Jim Elliot has a thought-provoking statement for us: "He is no fool, who gives what he cannot keep to gain what he cannot lose."[1]

Our race is to be and do all God calls us to! Up to this point, we've been exploring the aspect of doing—the plans God has for us and His desire for our lives to be productive. However, there is another dimension, one that actually takes precedence over our doing—and that is our being! Who we are is far more important than what we do. In fact, all we do is a natural outworking of who we are. What are God's goals for us in this arena?

If we are to be willing to pour ourselves into the race marked out for us, we need to understand clearly what the gold is in order to determine whether we want to give our all. In the Bible, a variety of goals are identified for us. To use another image, our goals are like the various facets of a diamond. The diamond itself represents Christ. Each facet is an aspect of becoming more like Him. In the questions that follow, these facets (goals) are enumerated. After exploring each section, identify the corresponding goal and fill in the appropriate blank.

Biblical Discovery and Reflection

*Goal #1:*_____

1. What was Christ's goal, or His reason in coming, according to John 3:16-17; 17:3-5, 24 (see also 1 John 3:1; 4:9-10)?

2. Our key passage, Hebrews 12:1-3, reveals that Jesus endured the cross on our behalf "for the joy set before him." This joy He was willing to die for was a love relationship with us! (This, then, becomes our first goal.)

    a. Why would this joy involve us rather than just His return to the Father?

    b. In *The Sacred Romance*, the authors write, "He ran 'for the joy set before him,' which means he ran out of *desire*. To use the familiar phrase, his heart was fully in it. We call the final week of our Savior's life his Passion Week. Look at the depth of his desire, the fire in his soul."[2] *We are His gold! We are why He ran His race here!* How does it impact you to know that *you* are His gold?

*Goal #2:*_____

3. What is God's goal for us in knowing Christ as our Savior, according to Paul in Galatians 4:19?

4. That this is God's heart for each of us is communicated by Christ's incarnation. Examine Luke 1:26-38.

   a. Whom did God desire to form within Mary?

   b. What response was necessary on Mary's part?

   c. Who then formed Jesus in her?

5. Another way Paul expresses this goal is found in Colossians 1:27-29.

   a. To what end does he wholeheartedly labor?

   b. J. Oswald Sanders, in *Enjoying Intimacy with God*, gives insight into this Colossians passage. He states:

   The Greek word for "maturity"—teleios—"an end, or goal, or limit," is rich in its significance. It combines two ideas: (a) the attaining of some standard, and (b) the achieving of some goal. . . . As Paul used the word, it meant "brought to completion, full-grown, lacking nothing.". . . Spiritual maturity, expressed in the simplest terms, is—*Christlikeness.*[3]

6. How does it impact you to know that the Lord desires to form Christ in you, bringing you into Christlikeness? What hope does this give you for who you are and for what He has for your life?

*Goal #3:*_____

7. As God's Spirit forms Christ in us and conforms us to His image, another goal of God's is accomplished within us. What is this other goal, according to Leviticus 20:7, 1 Corinthians 1:2, Hebrews 12:10, and 1 Peter 1:15-16.

    a. How do we often picture being holy? On what is your image of holiness based? Is holiness something you personally have desired? Why or why not?

    b. What insight does Jesus being holy give you about what holiness actually looks like?

    c. Oswald Chambers, in his devotional classic *My Utmost for His Highest*, states: "God's life in us expresses itself as *God's* life, not as human life trying to be godly."[4] What would be the differences in, and results of, both of these expressions?

    d. Andrew Murray, in *The Believer's Secret of Holiness*, provides further understanding:

        Our calling, before and above everything else, is to holiness. . . .
        . . . To be holy is to be Godlike, to have a disposition, a will, a character like God. . . .

. . . The quality is not something we do or attain: it is the communication of the divine life, the inbreathing of the divine nature, the power of the divine presence resting on us. And our power to become holy is to be found in the call of God: the Holy One calls us to himself that He may make us holy in possessing himself. . . .

. . . When God calls us to holiness, He calls us to himself and His own life.[5]

8. How is the secret to our holiness revealed and summarized in 1 Corinthians 1:30-31?

9. After considering the passages above, has your understanding changed regarding what it means to be holy? Explain. How has your desire for it changed?

Goal #4: _____

10. Because God is holy and fills us with Himself, what primary goal of His is increasingly accomplished? Consider Jesus' prayer in John 17:21, 26, along with the following reflections from devout Christians through the ages.

   a. Oswald Chambers states: "Jesus prayed nothing less for us than absolute oneness with Himself, just as He was one with the Father."[6]

   Chambers also proclaims: "From Jesus Christ's perspective, oneness with Him, with nothing between, is the only good thing."[7]

Succinctly, Chambers states: "God's purpose is to make us one with Himself."[8]

b.   St. Teresa of Avila, Madame Jeanne Guyon, St. John of the Cross, Dame Julian of Norwich, and others proclaimed union with Christ as our goal and God's deepest and highest desire for us and for Him. Calvin Miller, in presenting their writings, concludes:

> If any human life holds a reason to exist, the reason must be union with Christ. . . .
> . . . Our hungers should be those of union with Christ, not a hunger for merely knowing more about him or praising his goodness. . . . We truly are his joy and his crown. Union is his near obsession for all whom he loves.[9]

c.   How do these thoughts impact you, and what does the fact that so many proclaim this communicate to you?

11.   Oneness, and the intimacy that comes with it, is God's goal. He even gave us the image of marriage to better understand the relationship He desires with us. In the Old Testament, the Lord refers to Himself as His people's "Husband" (see Isa. 54:5; Hosea 2:16, 19-20). In the New Testament, Jesus is referred to as our "Bridegroom" (see Matt. 9:14-15, 25:1-10; John 3:27-30), and His church is referred to as His Bride (see Eph. 5:25-32.) Finally, Revelation reveals that this relationship with Him culminates with the "wedding" and the "wedding supper" (see Rev. 19:7-9). What is your response to God wanting this intimacy with you?

12.   Because He loves us so deeply, fully, and tenderly, what does God desire from us, according to Jesus in Matthew 22:37-38? Why would this mutuality be important to Him?

*Goal #5:*_____

13. As we love Him in return, what becomes our desire—and a goal—according to 2 Corinthians 5:8-9?

    a. How is this a natural outworking of love, as revealed in our earthly love relationships? What understanding do your human relationships give you of this desire toward our Lord?

    b. Amy Carmichael's prayer was: "O Lord Jesus, my Beloved, let me be a joy to Thee."[10] What does her prayer reveal of her heart for the Lord and the desire for her life?

*Goal #6:*_____

14. What else becomes our desire and is also a desire of God's for us? Consider John 17:10 and Ephesians 1:3-6.

15. This goal is summarized and clearly stated in the Westminster Catechism: "The chief end of man is to glorify God and enjoy Him forever." How would society today fill in the blank regarding what "the chief end of man" is?

The Gold: Christ Himself

16. Just as we are Christ's gold, *He* is ours! How does Paul reveal this in Philippians 3:7-8?

   a. What energy does Paul expend toward his goals in Christ (see verses 12-14)?

   b. Where was Paul's focus in life? Where were his eyes fixed?

17. It's so easy to have our focus be on us in our relationship with the Lord. Yet our focus should not be on what we can get *from* Him but rather our hunger and desire *for* Him! Then, delightfully, we find all else naturally follows. Has your primary desire been Christ, or has it been more what He can give you or do for you?

   a. A. W. Tozer writes: "God being who He is must always be sought for Himself, never as a means toward something else."[11]

   b. Calvin Miller reflects, "Knowledge may write theology, but only love can spell Union with Christ. . . . The longing of lovers is as near as I can get to explaining the kind of hunger that believers ought to feel for their separated Lord. . . . The yearning of some who walk with Christ is a dogging kind of hunger that is not willing to wait for eternal union. It wants to know Christ *now*."[12]

18. *Christ Himself is our gold! He* is the one for whom we run! We run toward Him to gain Him! He Himself is our treasure—worth sacrificing all! *Our race begins "with Him" and ends "in Him"!*

Personal Application and Response

19. Review the goals unveiled in this chapter. Record them here.

1.   4.   The Gold:
2.   5.
3.   6.

20. How do your goals correspond to those of God's for you? Next to the items above, rate each according to how important it is to you.

    a.   What did you discover? Is Christ this gold to you? What other things are you holding as the gold in your life?

    b.   On a scale of one to ten, how important is it for you to know Christ and nurture a love relationship with Him? What words describe your desire to know Him?

    c.   How would you describe the energy you are putting into gaining knowing Him better and deepening your oneness? What actions support your response?

21. Many things can distract and deter us in this race. An analogy can be drawn from a road trip my husband and I embarked on to San Diego to visit our son Scott, our daughter-in-law Stephanie, and our precious granddaughter Alexis. That was our goal—the "gold" for us was time with them. As we traveled, we experienced some parallels regarding some things that can happen as we journey toward Christ.

a. Road blocked! As we headed across I-40 toward Flagstaff, an accident ahead closed the highway. Many were stuck there for the night. Fortunately, we had our CB radio on and were alerted to it in time to go around it. As we travel toward Christ, sometimes we encounter a "roadblock." Perhaps something happens on our journey and we get stuck there. It's important to process our struggles with Him, so we can keep going. Is there anything that has become a "roadblock" for you? Talk with the Lord regarding anything keeping you stuck.

b. As we continued on our way, we came to Lake Havasu. What a beautiful area! It was tempting to just stay there. This can also happen in our journey toward Christ. We can become comfortable, enjoying where we are, and simply stop. Have you stopped seeking to know Christ better and experience Him more fully?

c. We also went through a dry, desert area. This parallels another thing that can happen in our journey in Christ. Occasionally, we can enter a period of dryness—a "desert" experience. Frequently in such times, we may tire of waiting to be met by the Lord and give up. How can we keep motivated to seek when God remains silent?

d. Another thing that can happen is forgetting the goal and getting sidetracked in our present circumstances. For example, on our trip we could have gone sight-seeing and forgotten where we were going. Using a different analogy, I think about dog racing. The dogs line up and the gates open. Fortunately for them, the track is clearly marked with fences or walls. But what if there wasn't anything keeping them in the race? Instead of heading to the finish line, they could take off after rabbits, for example. Or they might see a cat to chase or a pond to jump in. This can happen to us too. Life is like an undefined track. We're given birth and then told, "Go for it!" We may recognize God's call to a race, but we can get sidetracked—we can go chasing rabbits. Are there any "rabbits" you are chasing?

e. A final occurrence, however, might be that we simply give up. Perhaps we run into difficulty—"have car trouble"—and get discouraged in the journey. Or on the "long drive," we get tired. Perhaps the effort to keep growing simply feels too hard. For us, of course, on our road trip to San Diego, no matter how hard, how long, how many distractions, nothing was going to keep us from being with our kids and granddaughter! We had that gold clearly in mind. How can we keep Christ as our motivation to keep going when we get weary or things get rough?

f. How would you describe your journey toward Christ thus far? Have you been "chasing rabbits"? Have you become comfortable and settled somewhere nice along the way? Have you grown tired or disheartened in the journey? Or have you been steadily persevering toward your goals in Christ? Explain.

g.   Continuing with the analogy above, where are you now? Do you need "a course correction"? If so, what is that and how will you do so?

22. In *The Sacred Romance*, the authors issue this challenge:

> Will we leave our small stories behind and venture forth to follow our Beloved into the Sacred Romance? The choice to become a pilgrim of the heart can happen any day and we can begin our journey from any place. . . . "This life," wrote Jonathan Edwards, "ought to be spent by us only as a journey toward heaven." That's the only story worth living in now. The road goes out before us and our destination awaits. In the imagery of Hebrews, a race is set before us and we must run for all we're worth.[13]

a.   What is your response to the Lord's desire to nurture an intimate love relationship with you? What are your feelings as you contemplate growing in oneness with Him? Talk with Him regarding these.

b.   What truths can help you overcome any fears you have and encourage your desire for closeness?

c.   How would you describe your desire now to run for all you're worth?

23. In closing, review Paul's expression regarding the immeasurable worth of knowing Christ in Philippians 3:7-8, and the energy he was putting into gaining this gold. Express your own heart to the Lord.

🎣 Group Discussion Questions

1. In the introduction to this chapter, reference was made to Olympic athletes who give their all to achieve a gold medal. What strikes you about the effort believers put into pursuing the gold of Jesus Christ?

2. In life, can people go for the gold in several different areas, the Lord being one of them? Why or why not? What might they experience within by trying to do so? Of what value is focus?

3. Does it seem difficult to nurture "a marriage relationship" with the Lord? What questions, if any, does this concept raise for you? Do you think this relationship competes with other relationships in our lives—or does it enhance the others? Explain.

    What emotions surface as you consider the incredible love of the Lord for you?

5. Has this lesson made a difference in your desire to nurture a closer relationship with God? If so, in what ways? How will you do this?

Fix Your Eyes on Jesus

❧ 5 ❧

Throwing Off All That Hinders

In going for the gold, we are exhorted in our Hebrews 12 passage to "throw off everything that hinders." For runners in a physical race, this can represent extra body weight or even perhaps a heavy back-pack. Any unnecessary weight for athletes is a hindrance. To win their race, all excess baggage must be eliminated.

Evaluating these hindrances is critical to removing them. Dr. Jack Daniels, a world champion athlete whom *Runner's World* magazine calls the "world's greatest coach," states: "A race should be thought out, prepared for, and performed with determined intensity."[1] If we're serious about running the race we're called to for all we're worth, we need to think through what things, if any, are holding us back—hindering us—from being and doing all that God has pre-pared for us in Him. Then we can determine how to throw them off—so we can go for the gold!

To run well spiritually, it's even more important to do this, because our gold has eternal value and involves the very essence of life. What's holding us back from being our best and running well? What extra weight or old baggage are we carrying around? What hindrances do we need to determinedly throw off?

In the popular book *Body for Life*, Bill Phillips remarks that there came a time when "I made a conscious decision to change my life." After embarking on a diet and exercise program, he found, "I had more strength and energy . . . and even better than that, I had regained what I knew was my true character."[2] What a difference getting rid of extra weight can make! Today we, too, can make a conscious decision to change our lives spiritually. Are you willing to take a look at what might be hindering you? Are you willing to take action and throw these things off? To explore what some extra weight or hindering baggage can be, let's turn to God's Word.

Biblical Discovery and Reflection—Part One

1. What hindrances, if any, immediately come to mind in becoming all God created you to be, doing all He has prepared for you, and growing in the intimacy with Him that He desires? Record your thoughts here, then seek the Lord's help and direction as you proceed through this chapter.

2. One item in our "heavy backpack" can be *guilt!* How can this burden hinder us from moving out in what God has for us?

3. Is there anything we can do, say, feel, or think that would cause God to disqualify us or declare us ineligible to participate in His race? What are your initial thoughts?

4. For insight, consider David, God's anointed and appointed king of Israel. For a time, he was running well, but then he tripped up in a major way through his sins of committing adultery with Bathsheba and arranging the murder of her husband, Uriah.

   a. When David tried to hide what he had done, what were some of the results, according to Psalm 32:1-5?

b. Did God reject him from any further service? What did the Lord want David to do? What resulted from David's response?

5. The incredible truths of God's grace are powerfully evidenced in Manasseh's life. What sins did King Manasseh commit, recorded in 2 Chronicles 33:1-6, 9?

a. Yet what does it say the Lord did, according to verse 10?

b. When Manasseh turned to the Lord, how did the Lord respond to him (see verses 12-13)? How does Manasseh's experience encourage you?

c. From verses 13-17 what do you discover about Manasseh's "race"? Did God forgive him yet disqualify him from being king? How did Manasseh run his race following his return to the Lord? What lessons are here for us?

6. Jesus affirms that these truths certainly do apply to us. What was our condition when He gave His life for us, revealed in Romans 5:6-8? What does this communicate to you?

7. When we respond to God's love and grace, of what can we be assured, according to Romans 8:1? Personalize this truth—and give the Lord thanks!

Personal Application and Response—Part One

8. Although the Lord will not sever our *relationship* with Him due to willful behavior, our *fellowship* with Him can be damaged (as evidenced in David's life.) What hope is there for us when this occurs, according to 1 John 1:9?

9. Take time now for any needed cleansing and the restoring of rich fellowship with the Lord. On a separate piece of paper, record those offenses causing you guilt today. Confess them to Him, asking for His forgiveness and restoration.

    a. Of what can you be confident, according to the promise in 1 John 1:9 and Psalm 103:8-14?

    b. Jerry Bridges, in *Transforming Grace*, provides wonderful insight for us regarding this Psalm 103 passage. He writes:

    > Psalm 103:12 reads, "As far as the east is from the west, so far has he removed our transgressions from us." How far is the east from the west? If you start due north at any point on earth, you would eventually cross over the North Pole and start going south, but that is not true when you go east or west. If you start west and continue in that direction you will always be going west. North and south meet at the North Pole, but east and west never meet. In a sense, they are an infinite distance apart.[3]

    Reflect on this truth as it applies to you.

    c. Sheila Walsh differentiates guilt from shame. She states that guilt is "the feeling that accompanies having *done* something wrong," and shame is "the feeling that you are something wrong."[4] Do you struggle with shame? Why does Christ's grace free you from both of these?

d. In Lamentations 3:22-23, Jeremiah underscores these truths by proclaiming that God's mercies are "new every morning." Then he exclaims to the Lord, "Great is your faithfulness"! *Accept His grace now, and thank Him for His mercies that are new each morning for you!*

10. What is your conclusion, based on the passages in the lesson, regarding whether you can be disqualified from running God's race? (Note that the word *race* is the primary part of *grace.*)

11. Although we can throw off the guilt and shame that holds us back, sometimes we have trouble doing so! We accept God's forgiveness; but we continue to beat ourselves up. Our refusal to forgive ourselves becomes a heavy backpack in our race, which weighs us down!

a. Consider what would have happened had the Apostle Paul done that.

(1) Who was Paul and what did he do prior to being met by God in His grace? Read Acts 7:54-8:3 and 9:1-6.

(2) Did Paul's offenses disqualify him from the race? See Acts 13:1-3.

(3) What could Paul (Saul) have done with the rest of his life in response to recognizing the terrible mistakes he had been making?

(4) As Paul received God's grace and responded to God's call, however, he was used by God to preach throughout the Roman Empire, establish churches, and write follow-up letters that have become a significant part of God's Holy Word. Consider the consequences to the church had he not thrown off that guilt.

b.   The Enemy of Christ attempts to hinder us from running our race by sometimes whispering insidiously, "How could God use you after what you have done?" Satan wants to keep us in bondage, not wanting us to be free in Christ. Although we are forgiven, he tries to prevent us from living in that grace. Do you struggle with this? How can these truths, along with Paul's example, enable you not only to receive God's grace but in that grace to forgive yourself, throwing off that backpack of guilt and running wholeheartedly the race set before you?

c.   Take those steps now. First, thank the Lord for His grace. Then, throw off that backpack by saying out loud, "I receive Your grace, and in Your mercy I now forgive myself." Proclaim to Him now your willingness (if you so desire) to run the race He has called you to in Christ.

12.   In concluding the section of this first hindrance, read the incident recorded in Zechariah 3:1-5.

a.   Put yourself in Joshua's place. What is being portrayed here for you?

b.   *See yourself dressed in these clean clothes of Christ's righteousness.* Stand against the lies of the Enemy and run with perseverance the race marked out for you! Celebrate His grace daily! And keep your eyes fixed on Jesus!

Biblical Discovery and Reflection—Part Two

13. *Hurts from the past* are another major hindrance that we need to overcome. We live in a fallen, hurting world in which there is a lot of brokenness. The hurts we experience from the past (or present) can hinder us from freely moving out in all God calls us to.

   a. That God's heart is to heal us of these hurts is indicated by Jesus in John 7:23. What phrase does Jesus use to describe the healing He gives? Interestingly, the Latin root of the word *salvation* is *salus*, meaning "wholeness"! What does this communicate regarding God's desire for you?

   b. This truth is also communicated in who God proclaims He is. What does the Lord clearly state in Exodus 15:26?

   c. In addition to this being His name, I know this is who He is because I personally have experienced healing in His love. The home I grew up in was not a loving home. I realized later that my parents did love me, but due to their broken-ness, they were unable to show it. My mother had shut down emotionally due to pain both from her childhood and in her marriage. My father had severe emotional problems from pain he experienced as a child. Consequently, I never recall as a child being held or told that I was loved. In fact, I remember my father rebuking my younger brother for telling my dad that he loved him. In anger, my father turned on my little brother and commanded, "Don't you ever use that word again!"
   In addition to lack of love, there was volatile anger in our home. We never knew when my dad would erupt or what would trigger it. At times, his anger would be vented in the form of physical abuse, to me in particular; at other times, he would punish with cold silence for weeks.

But it was this desperate need to be loved fully and unconditionally that brought me to the Savior! As I understood *why* Christ died for me—because He *loved* me—I responded wholeheartedly to Him. As I soaked up this love, He brought healing deep within. Over the years, I have found that it is His love that brings healing to all my hurts. And this is His heart for each of us!

Personal Application and Response—Part Two

14. What is your story? Are you carrying any pain—for example, from your childhood relationships, from school incidents, from work, or in your marriage? What initially comes to mind, past or present?

15. What things might keep people from wanting to be healed and freed from these burdens? In considering this, read the incident of the man by the pool in John 5:1-9.

    a. Why would Jesus ask a paralyzed man if he wanted to be well? What reservations or fears might this person have had in being made whole and set free?

    b. What similar feelings might people have today regarding being healed of hurts and freed to run the race? What excuses do people frequently give for not participating in the race marked out for them?

    c. As Jesus asks you this question today, what is your response? Process your feelings with Him in your journal, being totally honest with Him. What truths about who He is and who He promises to be help you?

16. Jesus grieves with us over the pain we experience in this broken world, as His taking on Himself our sorrows on the cross shows

(Isa. 53:4-5). There is a song that beautifully communicates Jesus' heart for us in the pain we experience. The verse from that song follows. As you read this, hear Him speak these words tenderly to you today.

> And Jesus said, "Come to the water, stand by my side.
> I know you are thirsty, you won't be denied.
> I felt every teardrop when in darkness you cried.
> And I long to remind you that for those tears I died."[7]

17. With this in mind, bring to Him the hurts that cause you pain today, whether past or present, for He grieves with you in each you listed above. Because He loves you and died to bring you wholeness in Him, be assured that He meets you now as you come to Him. Spend time with Him, journaling your thoughts. In feeling your pain, pour out your heart to Him. Allow Him to meet you, comfort you, and speak His love to you. Receive His love! And remember, healing for deep hurts takes time. Keep coming and drinking of this living water, savoring His love for you. In time, your memories will no longer cause you pain or keep you from moving out in all He is calling you to be and do.

18. Amazingly, these hurts, "roadblocks," inefficiencies, can actually become part of our race. God is the Redeemer! My friend Janice is a wonderful example. Sexually and physically abused for years as a child, the Lord has brought her healing—and now she ministers to other survivors bringing them hope. How have you seen Him weave pain and hardship into something glorious and inspiring? What specific example can you give? How does this encourage you?

19. Having explored the two hindrances of guilt and hurt, review your responses in question 1. Were there any other hindrances that came to your mind that you need to throw off? (Some will be considered in the next chapter as well.) Bring any you

recorded to the Lord now. What truths can help set you free from these?

20. In concluding this lesson, review Paul's proclamation in Philippians 3:13-14. What was he doing regarding his past? What was his new passion?

   a. Are you willing to forget the past and keep your eyes fixed on the gold—on Christ Himself? Don't let anything take you out of the race. Grab that baton and press on to all God has called you to in Christ! Write out your heart's desire for this here, personalizing this Philippians passage for yourself.

   b. Then thank Him for His healing and freeing love!

✍ Group Discussion Questions

1. What are some reasons why people may not want to throw off the bondage of their guilt or the pain of their hurts? How have you seen this? Are there ways in which you struggle with this? If you would like, share your struggles with the others in the group and ask them to pray for you—and with you now—in this. (Group reminder: Always respect a person's wishes of confidentiality.)

2. Is it difficult to receive God's grace? As the Lord desires to dress us in clean, rich garments, do we resist? Why or why not? If we do, how can we overcome this?

3. Is it difficult to receive God's love? What obstacles can keep us from experiencing His love to the fullness He desires? Would

you care to share any ways in which you have personally experienced God's healing and freeing in your life?

4. How does understanding Paul's past make even more meaningful his proclamation in Philippians 3:13-14? How does this inspire you?

✥ 6 ✥

Forsaking the Sin That Entangles

"When you overcome resistance, you create the power to continually reach higher," states Bill Phillips in his book *Body for Life* regarding our physical fitness.[1] Spiritually this is true as well. The Bible encourages us in our race to "throw off everything that hinders and the sin that so easily entangles" (Heb. 12:1). Then we are able to run well and reach the heights we are called to in Christ.

Regarding these sins that entangle, the Apostle Paul exhorts Timothy (and us): "But you, man of God, flee from all this, and pursue righteousness, godliness, faith, love, endurance and gentleness. Fight the good fight of the faith" (1 Tim. 6:11-12). To pursue this course, let us come before the Lord openly and honestly as we turn to His Word.

Biblical Discovery and Reflection

1. What resistance might we have in overcoming sinful behavior in our lives? Do you sense any resistance within yourself now?

2. Merle Haggard sings a song titled "I Have No Reason for Livin' Right." What is our motivation for throwing off the sin that easily entangles? What especially helps you?

   a. Oswald Chambers, in his devotional *My Utmost for His*

Highest, writes: "God never tells us to give up things just for the sake of giving them up, but He tells us to give them up for the sake of the only thing worth having, namely, life with Himself. It is a matter of loosening the bands that hold back our lives."[2]

    b.   Reflect on Chambers' comments. How does fixing your eyes on Jesus motivate you?

3.   As we keep our eyes on Jesus, what are we called to do in 2 Corinthians 7:1, and why?

4.   In this spirit, read Colossians 3:1-14.

    a.   What offenses does Paul exhort us to "put to death" and "rid yourselves of"? List these below.

    b.   In addition, consider the attitudes or behaviors that are the *opposite* of the Christlike attributes Paul says we should cultivate. Identify those and record them below as well.

    c.   As you reflect on the lists above, which one(s) caused you to flinch as you read them? Which one(s), if any, did the Lord convict you on?

    d.   Are there any other sins or weaknesses in your life that trip you up as you desire to run your race?

    e.   Confess your sorrow over each specific sin to Him at this time. Review His promise to you in 1 John 1:9.

5.   We're exhorted to put these to death and rid ourselves of them, but can we do this in our own strength? What are your thoughts?

a. What war is going on within us, according to Romans 7:18-25? How do you identify with Paul?

b. According to Romans 7:25 with 8:9-11, where is our hope and help?

6. God's provision of strength for us in this battle is clarified in Hebrews 2:17-18 and 4:14-16. What did Christ experience? How successful was He?

a. When we receive Christ as our Savior, He Himself comes to live within us (Rev. 3:20)! Considering these verses in Hebrews, explain how it is possible for us to overcome temptation and be freed of sins that entangle.

b. To strengthen Christ's life in us, we need to feed on His Word. My friend Robin uses the following analogy to describe this war going on within us—and what makes the difference. She says it's like a tug-of-war between two horses: the dark horse represents our sinful nature, while the white horse represents the new life of Christ in us. Which one will win? The one you feed! In your battle, which one are you feeding? In what ways are you doing this?

7. Further encouragement is given in 1 Corinthians 10:13. What do you discover?

a. Can you give an example of this reality?

b. Consider your areas of weakness and vulnerability. What ways of escape are available to you in each? Be specific.

c. Bill Phillips states, "There is a world of difference between knowing what to do and actually doing it."[3] What is true physically here is also true spiritually. Determine now what you will do when tempted, and call on Christ's strength to help you take the way He is providing. Record your discoveries here.

8. Paul, in the Colossians 3:1-14 passage, addresses an issue that commonly seems to ensnare many believers. Because this concerns a critical dimension in our relationship with the Lord and with others, let's zoom in on it. Identify what this is by examining what Paul clearly exhorts us to do in Colossians 3:13, along with Ephesians 4:30-32.

9. If we choose not to forgive, how does this affect our Lord, as expressed in Ephesians 4:30? How does this impact you? Why would this also affect our fellowship with Him?

10. On what basis are we exhorted to forgive?

    a. How is this portrayed in Jesus' parable in Matthew 18:21-35? How does this speak to you personally?

    b. Sheila Walsh, in her book *Honestly*, shares from her own experience:

    As I began to forgive others, they returned to normal size. I no longer saw them in monster-like proportions. As long as I viewed someone as the enemy, I gave that person some power over my life. But as I forgave a person, I too was free. I saw that I could spend a lot of time imprisoned by past failures, or I could thank God for his never-ending grace and forgiveness and get on with the rest of my life.

    This took me back to the lesson from Jesus' parable of the unmerciful servant. I had been forgiven much—and I was to continue to reach out to others with the grace God had offered me.[4]

c. From my own experience, I, too, have discovered how I am kept in bondage if I refuse to forgive. The other person moves on with his or her life. I am the one who continues to suffer! When I choose to forgive, I am set free. Also, it gives me joy knowing I please the Lord by doing so.

11. The Lord cares deeply about the pain we experience in this world. As He exhorts us to forgive those who have hurt us, He has our good in mind. There are many ways in which harboring anger and bitterness adversely affects us, which we will explore. One way is that it can affect us physically. On "The Saturday Early Show" in March 2000, Dr. Emily Senay advised all to forgive, explaining that not forgiving affects our health! Why do you think this would be true?

12. What danger spiritually is there in harboring anger and bitterness, according to Ephesians 4:26-27 and 2 Corinthians 2:10-11? What is your reaction to this realization?

a. I saw this reality in my father's life. He tenaciously held on to offenses from the past. He became consumed with anger and was very bitter. When I approached him one day to forgive, he responded vehemently, "I have every right to be angry!" This anger opened the door to Enemy involvement in his life. This resulted in a lack of inner peace. He seemed tormented throughout his life, even on his deathbed.

b. Not forgiving has its price. Yet why do you think people might want to hang on to their anger?

c. Some people feel we are saying that what the offender did was okay if we forgive. Is that true? Does the Lord overlook another's sin? Whose actions are we responsible for? Can you entrust that one to the Lord, as you obey Him in your actions by forgiving?

13. In addition to when we experience hurt from another, we also have a choice in how we respond when painful circumstances occur.

   a. This is clearly seen in Naomi's experience in the book of Ruth in the Old Testament. Naomi's name meant "pleasant." But when over time her husband and both sons died, she became angry at God and changed her name to "Mara," which means "bitter" (see Ruth 1:20-21). When we feel angry with the Lord over something that has happened in our lives, what should we do with our anger? What choice did Naomi make?

   b. My friend Carol's husband was killed in a plane crash, leaving her with three children. Her prayer at that time was, "Lord, don't let this make me bitter." And the Lord then worked within her to not let that happen. As a result, she has deep peace within and a beautiful countenance as well.

   c. Traumatic circumstances may impact our lives, but they don't have to destroy our spirits. What do you learn from the examples above regarding our role in determining how these occurrences will affect our spirits?

14. Do you think there is there anything too severe, too great, to forgive? What are your initial thoughts?

   a. What do you learn from Christ's example? Read meditatively the passages below, recording the offenses committed against Jesus.

      Luke 22:54-65
      Luke 23:32-41

   b. What did Jesus pray in 23:34?

c. I have seen the Lord enable a believer to forgive the seemingly impossible. Phyllis J.'s son and his new wife were both sexually assaulted, beaten, and killed by a random murderer. She was the one who found them. As gruesome and painful as this was, she, over time, was able to forgive. That she has truly done so is evidenced in her spirit and on her countenance. She radiates peace and joy.

15. How is such forgiveness possible? Look at Stephen's experience as he was being stoned to death, recorded in Acts 7:54-60.

   a. How is Stephen described in verse 55?

   b. What does he pray in verse 60?

   c. What insight do these verses give regarding the key in being enabled to forgive?

Personal Application and Response

16. What offenses are causing you pain today? Record these below or in your journal. (Consider those you identified in chapter 5.)

    a. What has been your response to these hurts? Have you been brooding over the offense? Are you harboring anger toward the offender? Or have you been seeking God's healing and choosing to forgive? Be specific regarding each hurt listed.

    b. Do you have any fears in forgiving? Do you struggle with any reasons why you do not want to forgive?

    c. What discoveries so far in the lesson speak to you particularly in the choices you are making? What is your desire regarding each now?

17. In review, by choosing to forgive, you will:

    a. Please the Lord (or not "grieve" Him) and glorify Him.

    b. Not give the offender the satisfaction of wounding you for life.

    c. Not harm your health.

    d. Become set free to truly live your life.

18. Some helpful steps in the forgiving process are listed below. Spend some time now with the Lord as you process these for each hurt experienced. Repeat these steps as the hurt resurfaces—until the pain is gone and you are free.

    a. First, feel the pain of the offense. Ask the Lord to hold you and comfort you as you do so. Then ask the Lord to heal each hurt in His love. If we have buried the pain, it's important to acknowledge and feel it for healing to occur. As He brings healing, this helps us to forgive.

b. Reflect on the forgiveness and mercy you have received from Christ. We may think the one who offended us doesn't deserve to be forgiven, but how does reflecting on your forgiveness in Christ help you in this? Keep your eyes fixed on Him.

c. Ask for the Lord's insight and understanding of the offender. Not that this excuses him or her, but it does help give compassion and grace as we glimpse that person's pain.

d. Entrust yourself and what happened to "him who judges justly" (1 Peter 2:19-23) .

e. Ask the Lord to redeem what happened, using it for His good purposes (Rom. 8:28). Just as God used the evil Joseph's brothers intended against him for good, so the Lord can use the offenses against us for good. This, too, helps us forgive.

f. Ask for the enabling of His Spirit. Spend time with Him, nurturing His Spirit in you.

g. Choose to forgive out of obedience to the Lord. Say out loud, "In the name of Jesus, I forgive." Repeat as necessary.

19. Regarding other sins that entangle, how does it impact you to know that those sins you may struggle with dishonor the Lord, grieve Him, and hurt your relationship with Him? Express your heart to the Lord regarding these.

    a. If you find you really don't want to let go of any of the things you may have been convicted of through this lesson, come honestly to the Lord in this. Start where you are. Ask Him to help you want to want His help in overcoming a particular sin. He can't meet us and help us if we're not honest about where we really are.

    b. How does fixing your eyes on Jesus help you want to kick that bad habit or forsake that sin which dishonors and displeases your Lord? What higher longings stir within you as you see Him and know His desires for you?

    c. How will you draw on Christ's strength in withstanding specific temptations or in turning from any ungodly attitudes?

    d. What steps will you now take in overcoming other "sins that so easily entangle" you in your walk with the Lord? Address each specifically.

20. In closing, review Hebrews 12:1-2a: "Therefore, since we are surrounded by such a great cloud of witnesses, let us throw off everything that hinders and the sin that so easily entangles, and let us run with perseverance the race marked out for us. Let us fix our eyes on Jesus." Will you commit to doing so now? Express this to the Lord. To help you, write these verses out on a separate note card. Post it somewhere prominent as a continual reminder, and make this your daily prayer.

Group Discussion Questions

1. If someone continually repeats an offense, does continually forgiving them mean we are not to deal with the problem? Explain. Can you give an example?

2. What are some fears people may have in forgiving another? What truths address these fears? One common fear regarding forgiving an offender in a broken relationship is that people think forgiveness automatically means restoration. Do you think this is synonymous? Support your response.

3. What are some reasons why people may not want to forgive another? How can these reasons for resistance specifically be overcome? Can you give examples?

   a. What toll have you seen an unforgiving spirit take?

   b. What benefits of forgiveness have you seen or experienced?

4. What are some other common sins of the spirit that prove to be snares for believers? Would you care to share one you particularly struggle with?

5. Are we the only one affected by our sinfulness? How does our behavior or our attitudes affect others? Consider your family, coworkers, the church, nonbelievers, and even Christ Himself. Can you give examples? How does understanding the further implications of what we do and who we are help in overcoming these offenses?

6. What impacted you most powerfully from this lesson, and why?

❧ 7 ❧

Training for the Race

Physical fitness is a passion of our society today. For years, health clubs and fitness centers have been popular, with people even hiring their own personal trainers. The most recent trend is having specially designed exercise rooms in our homes. Proper nutrition is also part of this emphasis. Along with exercise books, nutrition and diet books comprise a major section of local bookstores and are the focus of many educational programs on television. Physical fitness seems to have become our national obsession!

No doubt about it, physical well-being is very important. Personally, I have a simple exercise program and also enjoy hiking with my husband. I was aware of how important keeping fit physically is when we were hiking one day to the Alpine tunnel by the Collegiate Peaks mountain range of Colorado. I kept needing to stop and rest (due to the altitude of course)—when who passed me but an eighty-four-year-old woman! That was humbling! As we were commending her fitness, she told us that when she was sixty she backpacked by herself for ten days in the High Sierras, a 12,000-foot range in California. Keeping fit was certainly paying off for her!

Athletes are disciplined people. Time for exercise is scheduled into their days, and is protected as a priority. As Christians called to run well in God's race, we can learn a lot from these athletes—for as important as physical fitness is, spiritual fitness is of greater value. In 1 Timothy 4:7-8, Paul writes: "Train yourself to be godly. For physical training is of some value, but godliness has value for all things, holding promise for both the present life and the life to come." Wow!

How critical spiritual training is.

As our nation obsesses on our bodies, sadly it seems our spirits are often neglected. Yet what is spiritual training? What disciplines need to be incorporated in our days and held as a priority? As we explore these spiritual disciplines in our training, please note that these disciplines are not obligations but rather are opportunities. These are means provided by God that we might know Him better and grow closer to Him. Jerry Bridges, in *Transforming Grace*, provides an important perspective for us as we consider these disciplines: "Spiritual disciplines are provided for our good, not for our bondage. They are privileges to be used, not duties to be performed. To take off on a familiar quotation from Jesus, 'Spiritual disciplines were made for man, not man for spiritual disciplines' (see Mark 2:27)."[1] With this perspective, let's turn to God's manual on fitness for insight.

Biblical Discovery and Reflection

1. Reflect on 1 Timothy 4:7-8 in the introduction above. Read it in several different versions. How does this speak to you? Be specific.

2. Many aspects of physical training parallel spiritual training. One such similarity has to do with nutrition. Athletes carefully watch their diet and feed on certain "energy foods." Bill Phillips, in *Body for Life* states: "When you nourish your body with pure energy, you transform from the inside out."[2] What spiritual parallel can you draw from his statement?

3. Before races, runners in the past were encouraged to do "carbo-loading." Carbohydrates produce energy, because once ingested they convert into glucose, or sugar. So athletes would load up on pasta, for example, the evening prior to a race. Bread is also a carbohydrate. For spiritual parallels, consider who Jesus

claims to be in John 6:32-35. What does this communicate to you regarding being spiritually fit?

a. What sustains and energizes us spiritually, according to Jesus in Matthew 4:4? What does this mean practically for you?

b. As good nourishment transforms the body, what occurs for us spiritually as we ingest God's Word, according to 1 Thessalonians 2:13?

c. What do these insights communicate to you regarding the importance of spending time in God's Word, whether we feel like it or not?

d. Darien Cooper, in *The Beauty of Beholding God*, shares her personal experience as she voraciously consumed God's Word and meditated on it throughout the day:

> Exciting things began to happen. As I chewed on the written Word, the Spirit caused it to become the Living Word within, adding flesh to my spiritually undernourished body. For awhile I held on to the Word because I knew it was my life support. Then I continued to hold on because it was my joy, my nourishment, and my fulfillment.[3]

How does her experience echo Jeremiah's in Jeremiah 15:16?

e. Have you previously thought of God's Word as the food your spirit thrives on? How does this insight motivate you to feed on Jesus and His Word regularly?

4. "The Disciplines allow us to place ourselves before God so that He can transform us," states Richard Foster in *Celebration of*

Discipline.[4] In addition to feeding on God's Word, what are we exhorted to do in Colossians 4:2?

a. Foster writes, "Prayer is the central avenue God uses to transform us."[5] He states: "The primary purpose of prayer is to bring us into such a life of communion with the Father that, by the power of the Spirit, we are increasingly conformed to the image of the Son."[6]

b. In addition, Oswald Chambers comments that if a person does not pray,

> What will suffer is the life of God in him, which is nourished not by [physical] food but by prayer. . . . Prayer is other than meditation; it is that which develops the life of God in us. When a person is born from above, the life of the Son of God begins in him, and he can either starve that life or nourish it. Prayer is the way the life of God is nourished.[7]

c. In our Colossians passage above, Paul exhorts us to *devote* ourselves to prayer! Richard Foster, in another book titled simply *Prayer*, comments: "Do we really think we can experience integration of heart and mind and spirit with an erratic prayer life? . . . We develop intimacy by regular association."[8] Is intimacy with God your desire? Will you *devote* yourself to prayer?

d. Regarding the dimension of powerful praying, Foster encourages us not to be overwhelmed and intimidated by "giants of the faith." He says that

> we should remember that God always meets us where we are and slowly moves us along into deeper things. Occasional joggers do not suddenly enter an Olympic

marathon. They prepare and train themselves over a period of time, and so should we. When such a progression is followed, we can expect to pray with greater authority and spiritual success a year from now than at present.[9]

How does this encourage you?

    e.   Is prayer a priority for you? Why or why not? Process your responses with the Lord, because He knows any struggles you may have with this. Express your heart to Him.

5.   Another area of spiritual training involves the disciplines of what we look at and think on.

    a.   The first dimension is what we look at because that often affects what we think on. What does Jesus reveal in Luke 11:34-36? What is He saying to us here?

    b.   The second dimension is addressed by Paul in Philippians 4:8. What does he exhort us to do?

    c.   When our thoughts are detrimental to our well-being, what are we told to do in 2 Corinthians 10:5? What do you think this means, and how do we do this? Can you give an example?

    d.   Is there anything you "look at" or "think on" that is detrimental for you in your walk with the Lord? If so, what will you do about it? Be specific.

6.   Another discipline in our spiritual training is spending time with the Lord in worship and loving fellowship. Oswald Chambers states: "A private relationship of worshiping God is the greatest essential element of spiritual fitness."[10]

a. How much a part of your time with the Lord is spent worshiping, adoring, and simply enjoying His presence?

b. How can we worship more both in our times with Him as well as through our day? Give specific tips and tools for worship.

7. Jesus states that it is essential that we abide in Him (John 15:4-11.) In previous chapters, the discipline of spending time with Him has been emphasized. It is the key to all dimensions of the Christian life.

a. If you haven't set aside a block of time each day to commune with the Lord, would you like to do so? Examine your schedule. Determine how much time is realistic for you and when the best time is. If finding this time is difficult, ask the Lord to show you what can be rearranged—or what needs to be eliminated. When will you, or do you, take this time?

b. J. Oswald Sanders, in his book *Enjoying Intimacy with God*, declares:

Both Scripture and experience teach that it is we, not God, who determine the degree of intimacy with Him that we enjoy. We are at this moment *as close to God as we really choose to be.* True, there are times when we would *like* to know a deeper intimacy, but when it comes to the point, we are not prepared to pay the price involved. The qualifying conditions are more stringent and exacting than we are prepared to meet; so we settle for a less demanding level of Christian living. . . . Intimacy is deepened by discipline.[11]

What is your response to his remarks? Does the level of intimacy you currently experience with Christ support this?

8. As we go through our day, we are to continue to commune with God. Frank Laubach and Brother Lawrence's discoveries in this are recorded in a book titled *Practicing His Presence*. Laubach writes, "I must learn a continuous silent conversation of heart to heart speaking with God while looking into other eyes and listening to other voices. . . . This simple practice requires only a gentle pressure of the will. . . . It grows easier as the habit becomes fixed. . . . It transforms life into heaven." Then Brother Lawrence comments, "I have found that we can establish ourselves in a sense of the presence of God by continually talking with Him."[12] Will you develop this habit of conversing with the Lord as you go through your day? Record your discoveries as this becomes an increasing part of your experience.

9. As we "practice His presence" and yield to Him throughout our day, what is another discipline in our training discerned from John 14:23-24 (see also 1 John 5:2-3)? Give an example of how to exercise this discipline. As we obey Him, what does this communicate to the Lord?

10. Richard Foster explains why obedience is a "discipline":
    > In the beginning our will is in struggle with God's will. . . .
    > In time, however, we begin to enter into a grace-filled releasing of our will and a flowing into the will of the Father. . . .
    > *Here we have the complete laying down of human will.* . . . Our relinquishment is a full and wholehearted agreement with God that his way is altogether right and good. . . .
    > . . . Relinquishment brings to us a priceless treasure: *the crucifixion of the will.* . . .
    > "The death of my own will"—strong language. But all of the great devotional masters have found it so. . . . Crucifixion always has resurrection tied to it. God is not destroying the will but transforming it so that over a

process of time and experience we can freely will what God wills.[14]

What resistance can people have to this concept?

11. Hannah Whitall Smith explains further this issue of the "death of our will":

> I am convinced that throughout the Bible the expressions concerning the "heart" do not mean the emotions but the will. . . . The object of God's dealings with an individual is that this "I" may be yielded up to Him and this central life abandoned to His control. . . .
>
> But let us not make a mistake here. I say we must "give up" our wills, but I do not mean we are to be left will-less. We are not to give up our wills and be left like limp nerveless creatures, without any will at all. We are simply to substitute for our misdirected wills . . . the higher, divine, mature will of God.[15]

What further understanding does this impart?

a. How do we discipline ourselves in this as we walk with the Lord each day? Can you give an example?

b. As we do so, Andrew Murray explains what results: "The Spirit teaches me to yield my will entirely to the will of the Father. . . . He reveals to me how union with God's will is union with God Himself."[16] Meditate on this truth.

Personal Application and Response

12. At times, to pursue growing in Christ and experiencing all He

has for us is a sheer act of discipline and will—out of our love for our Lord. Calvin Miller, in *Walking with Saints*, encourages us in this as he states:

> Discipline is the believer's part in the conversation of holy faith. When God speaks to us, he speaks grace. When we talk to God, we speak discipline. I'm forever telling my students that grace is God's gift to us and discipline is our gift to God. . . . As you "press toward the goal," your own discipline is your offering of love. . . . Remember, *discipline* and *disciple* both come from the same word.[17]

For further study of the disciplines in nurturing an intimate relationship with the Lord, see the author's study *At Jesus' Feet*.

b. Dietrich Bonhoeffer strongly states: "Salvation without discipline is merely cheap grace. It is a poor attempt to buy the most of God with the least of our yielding."[18] Reflect on this. What is your response?

c. In review, list the various disciplines studied in this lesson. Add to it any others you are aware of or practice yourself. As you consider each, reflect on how much a part of your day these disciplines are. Which one(s) do you desire to nurture more?

13. In both physical and spiritual training, *motivation* makes the difference. Too often, believers think of time apart with the Lord as spiritual obligation or a way to gain God's favor. On a scale of one to ten, how would you identify your motivation in the past, with one being "total love or desire" and ten being "obligation only"? Reflect on the following questions as well.

a. How motivated are you to experience all that God has for you and become all He desires for you to be in Him? Express your heart to Him.

b. How passionate are you in your desire to know Him better? If this has waned in you, ask the Lord to reignite within you this passion and fan it into flame!

14. Another dimension to our training is having "personal trainers," just as athletes have! We as believers can have personal spiritual directors or mentors to help guide us in our unique journeys. These are people who have walked ahead of us, who come alongside and give guidance, pointing us to Christ. Is there someone whose walk with the Lord you respect, with whom you would like to arrange specific times to meet? Pray about this, and if you sense God leading you, then call that individual to see if that would work in his or her schedule. This is a supportive and encouraging role we as the body of believers can have for one another.

15. *These disciplines are means to an end—Christ Himself.* A. W. Tozer reinforces this truth. He states: "The teaching of the Bible is that God is Himself the end for which man was created."[21] As you conclude this chapter, what are your desires?

16. Calvin Miller remarks in *Walking with Saints*, "The Bible is the story of God working through anybody who would treasure his presence." If this is our desire, God in essence says, "Stand back and watch what you will do as you treasure my company and practice my presence!"[22] In conclusion, personalize Ephesians 3:16-21, and make it your prayer. Write these verses out on a 3-by-5 card, carry them with you, and meditate on them. Ask the Lord to then do in you all that these Scriptures proclaim—for your joy and His glory!

Group Discussion Questions

1. Why does it seem to be easier to commit to physical training than

it does to spiritual training? How can these obstacles be overcome? How does realizing the value of time with the Lord help you be more motivated to set time apart daily to be with Him?

2. Just as when we commit to exercise programs, things will occur to keep us from those times, or circumstances can discourage us from persevering. Similarly, when a person commits to pursuing Christ, the Enemy will often attempt to prevent or discourage that person from spending time with the Lord. He will also attempt to keep that one from yielding to the Lord more fully. What are some of Satan's common tactics in these regards? Are there any you particularly struggle with? For starters, consider the oft-quoted remark ascribed to the Enemy to his agent, "If you can't make them bad, make them busy."

3. How do we resist giving up our wills? Why is this surrender, this relinquishment, important if we are to experience the fullness of all God has for us? How can the struggles in this battle be overcome? Be specific.

4. How can competition, which we experience every day in our world, hinder us in the race Christ calls us to in Him? What dangers are there in having a competitive attitude toward others? As we pursue our Lord, what should be our attitude toward others? Explain. What do you think the results would be of the various attitudes?

❧ 8 ❧

Running in Christ

As you have been running your race, have you been working up a sweat? (Excuse me—are you "perspiring"?) But seriously, has the Christian life felt burdensome? Many believers walk around as if the weight of the race is on their shoulders. Have you felt it's all been up to you in your particular race? You ask for God's help, but does it still feel heavy?

We can easily become intense and feel the pressure to perform well in a race that's supposed to glorify God. It seems many believers feel the Christian life is just a religious form of behavior modification. That can feel not only heavy, but also defeating as we try to improve ourselves to no great avail. Yet we read in the Bible that Jesus says His yoke is easy and His burden is light. Is that the way it feels to you? God's Word proclaims wonderful truths that can release us from pressure and enable us to run freely. To explore these, let's turn now to the Holy Scriptures.

Biblical Discovery and Reflection

1.   At this point in your life, how do you view becoming the person God wants you to be and producing the good results He desires from your life? Have you been carrying the responsibility in these areas? How have you been living this out, and how has it felt to you?

2. The secret for both areas is revealed in Paul's proclamation in Galatians 2:20. What does he reveal here as the secret of his life?

   a. When Paul states that "Christ lives in me," he uses the active verb *lives*. What is Paul actually proclaiming here (see also Rom. 8:9-11)?

   b. If you have received Christ as your personal Savior, what does it mean to you that Christ Himself by His Spirit is *alive* in you? Meditate on this awesome truth.

3. For the application of this truth, let's first consider what this means in the "being" dimension—becoming Christlike—since this is one of God's primary desires for us. Have you believed that it was up to you to make yourself into the best Christian you could for God?

   a. Read Galatians 5:22-23. As you read this list, have you asked God for patience, for example? Or have you determined to work at becoming more patient? Who does it say these qualities belong to?

   b. Thinking it's up to us to make ourselves Christlike is an easy trap to fall into. In fact, those in Galatia to whom Paul was writing had taken this on as theirs to do. What does Paul say to them in Galatians 3:1-3?

   c. As a new believer, I was under this impression. I realized I had been born anew by God's Spirit, but then I felt it was up to me to attain my goal of Christlikeness. I actually thought I was doing a pretty good job of it too. In fact, I realized later I had even become proud of the Christian I was making myself into! The Lord took me through some experiences that revealed all this to me. After stripping me of all I had made of myself, He brought me down to the foundation He laid in me of Jesus Christ. Then it was as though He said, "Now let *Me* do the building." Wow. How much freer! And so much better! Then *He* is the one glorified.

d. Actually, what does the Bible say about our ability to make ourselves righteous in Isaiah 64:6?

e. Watchman Nee addresses this truth of "Christ in us" in his book *Christ the Sum of All Spiritual Things.* He writes:

> Christianity is not reward, neither is it what Christ gives to me. Christianity is none other than Christ himself.
> Do you perceive the difference? These are two totally divergent ways. Christianity is not any one thing which Christ gives to me; Christianity is Christ giving himself to me. . . .
> . . . God has not granted us humility and patience and gentleness, He grants the entire Christ to us. It is Christ who becomes our humility, patience, gentleness. It is Christ, the living Lord. And this is what is truly called Christianity.[1]

Is this a new perspective to you? How does this reality impact you?

4. The truth of who conforms us to Christ is also proclaimed in 2 Corinthians 3:18. Review this passage meditatively.

a. What truths are revealed about our transformation?

b. What are our responsibilities—and what are not?

c. What is your response to these truths? Express your heart to the Lord regarding your desire for your life.

5. As the Spirit of Christ produces the fruit of the Spirit in us, what about the fruit God desires to be borne through us? Consider now this other dimension in the race marked out for us—that of "doing" those works prepared in advance for us (Eph. 2:10).

   a. Have you felt burdened to accomplish the results in what God calls you to do? Review the truths Jesus proclaims in John 15:4-5.

   b. Reflect on the analogy Jesus is using. What is He communicating? For example, consider how fruit actually appears on the branch of a tree. What is this saying to you personally?

   c. This principle of life is true both in the natural realm as well as in the spiritual. Just as life flows up through a fruit tree into the branches and naturally produces fruit, so as Christ's life flows through us, eternal fruit is naturally produced!

6. Why must it be Christ who accomplishes His purposes in us (see John 3:6)? What do you discover (see also 1 Cor. 3:5-13)?

   a. Many hardworking Christians have made this discovery and have been set free. In addition, their lives have become increasingly productive. One person is W. Ian Thomas, who was a major in the British army during World War II and later became a missionary. Initially, though, he was having little success when he shared the Gospel. Finally, he wept in despair and felt that, unless something changed, he could not go to the mission field. As he poured his heart out to the Lord, God opened his eyes to the truth that "Christ is our life!" Thomas wrote of his experience:
      "It just came from every area of God's Word, and very kindly and very lovingly the Lord seemed to make it

plain. . . . : 'You see, for seven years, with utmost sincerity, you have been trying to live *for* Me, on My behalf, the life that I have been waiting for seven years to live *through* you. . . . You have been busy trying to do *for* Me all that only I can do *through* you.'" . . .

Christian friends began to notice that something was different in the life of God's young servant. He met Christians who were as weary and exhausted as he had been, and he was able to share with them the secret of the Life. . . . He and they were making the discovery of that fullness of life in Christ Himself, and only in Him.[2]

b. How did Jesus model this for us, revealed in His proclamation in John 14:10? How does this discovery impact you?

c. Watchman Nee endorses these truths by stating clearly: "Divine work can only be done with divine power, and that power is to be found in the Lord Jesus alone."[3]

d. What are your reactions to the above proclamations and discoveries?

e. Why are these freeing truths? What understanding does this give you of Jesus' words, "My yoke is easy, my burden is light" (Matt. 11:30)?

7. As we recognize how critical it is to "run *in* Christ," we grasp more fully why it is important not to push with our wills and purposes.

a. What things can influence us to take things on as ours?

b. I can tell the difference when I am moving in Him and when I've taken over. When I'm abiding, there is peace. When I'm not, I sense I'm pushing—or I'm a little anxious or uptight. Realizing that our race is run in Him, we can learn an important lesson from car racing (like the Indy 500). In these races, when danger on the track occurs, a yellow flag is waved, warning the drivers to be alert and take caution. For me, anxiety or feeling burdened for results is this caution flag. These feelings warn me that I have taken something on as mine! It alerts me to that danger. When I give it back to the Lord as His, peace returns as I rest in the truth that He will be faithful to accomplish His purposes. What can you identify as "caution flags" for you? How can being alert to these help you?

c. It can be very tempting to do things in self rather than in Him. If the Lord reveals a specific purpose for you, one of the hardest things to do is "wait" for His timing and His way. Abraham is a classic example. What did he do, and what resulted? Read Genesis 15:4-6 and 16:1-13; 17:15-22 and 21:1-2. What lessons speak to you from Abraham's experience? Can you relate this to your life? Explain.

d. What is the difference in being responsible *in* a task and responsible *for* it?

8. From the example of Abraham above, what do you learn of God's ability to fulfill His purposes? Apply this to His purposes for you.

9. Are we on our own for the other demands that life puts on us; or do these truths also apply to all areas of life? What are your initial thoughts?

a. What insight do you gain from the following passages?

Isaiah 40:29-31
Philippians 4:19
Colossians 2:3 and James 1:5

b. What does Paul clearly say in Philippians 4:13?

c. Corrie ten Boom experienced the truth of Christ's life in us when she was in a concentration camp in World War II. She writes of this discovery when she and her sister Betsie were overwhelmed with their circumstances.

> Betsie leaned against her beloved sister and whispered, "Oh, Corrie, this is hell."
> Courage is born in adversity, but Corrie said she was not brave, that she often pulled her dirty blanket over herself and prayed, "Lord I am weak and cowardly and of little faith; hold me close. Thou art the conqueror. Give me courage." From that dependence, that surrender to her Lord, Corrie accomplished feats that were astounding for a woman in her fifties, weakened by malnutrition and ill-treatment.[4]

d. To experience the fullness of God's resources, what are our responsibilities? Be specific. Support with an example.

10. All of these truths are summed up in a key verse: Acts 17:28. Dissect this verse. What is being communicated?

a. As explored in chapter 4, the desire of God's heart for us is union with Himself. How does Acts 17:28 capture this truth?

b. Madame Jeanne Guyon beautifully portrays these truths with the following simile: "As a torrent empties into the sea, its waters can be distinguished from the sea for quite a long time, but gradually the waters of this river mix with the sea completely." In essence, she states that we are like this river. The further we flow into Christ, the more complete our oneness becomes. As this occurs, she says our individuality is not lost, but quite the opposite. Each of us, she says, is "truly set free to be who [we] really are."[5]

c. Meditate on these truths. What do they communicate to you regarding the truths of "running our race in Him?" How do they impact you personally?

Personal Application and Response

11. Summarize the truths explored in this lesson of (1) Christ alive in us for our "being," and (2) of Christ's life flowing through us for our "doing." Explain why it is essential that it be His life, His power, not our efforts.

12. Reflect on the following questions:

a. Have you been laboring at making yourself into the best Christian you can be? If so, how has that felt?

b. Have you been taking on the responsibility of results in the tasks the Lord calls you to? Has that been a pressure and burden to you?

c. Which statement best describes how you have been living thus far: "I am living my life for Christ," or "Christ is living His live out through me"? Which way would you like to live?

d. How would you describe your running generally? Are you most frequently running from Him, to Him, with Him, ahead of Him, or in Him?

13. Have you wondered where the joy is you hear about in Christ? What insights do you now have regarding this?

14. What truths in this lesson set you free?

15. What changes, if any, would you like to make in the running of your race? How will you do so? Explain.

16. How will you draw on His resources, His life in you, for the demands on you due to circumstances or relationships? Be specific.

17. As David abided in the Lord, he proclaimed his discoveries of the Lord of the race. What truths does he record in Psalm 18:30-33? How do these realities for David apply to you?

    a.   Hannah Hurnard springboards off of David's expressions in her allegory *Hinds' Feet on High Places*. She writes:

> A hart, followed by a hind, had appeared from among the jumbled rocks around them and were now actually beginning to ascend the precipice. . . .
> . . . The hart would leap across the gap and go springing upward, always closely followed by the hind, who set her feet exactly where his had been, and leaped after him, as lightly, as sure-footed, and apparently unafraid as it was possible for any creature to be. So the two of them leaped and sprang with perfect grace and assurance up the face of the precipice and disappeared from sight over the top.[6]

    b.   As you consider the heights to which the Lord is taking you in Him, express your heart to Him now regarding how you desire to live in Him and with Him.

Group Discussion Questions

1. What are the contrasts from how the world says we are to run our races and how the Lord reveals we are to run? How do these messages from the world often influence our Christian lives?

2. What questions do you have regarding any of the truths in this lesson? What new insights did you gain?

3. What are the felt differences we will experience as we run more in Him, as opposed to trying to do everything ourselves? Can you share examples?

4. What hope does this lesson give you for your "being" and for your days? Explain.

5. How do the truths of this lesson excite you about the Lord? Is He bigger and better than you had previously thought? Explain. How do your discoveries motivate you to grow closer and deeper into Him? What will you do about it? Be specific.

❧ 9 ❧

Persevering When
the Race Gets Tough
Part One: Understanding God's Purposes

A cross-country race covers many types of terrain. In Colorado, such a race takes runners on trails alongside beautiful, still mountain lakes as well as up relatively unmarked, rocky, barren heights. There are times in the thin mountain air, when the sun burns hot and the course is rough, that a runner is tempted to give up. It is then that one must keep in mind the goal and understand the values of that challenge.

Just as we can experience a journey across such terrain in a physical race, there can be times in life when the way becomes unmarked, rocky, and barren. Difficult times will come, for we live in a fallen world. In such times, we have choices to make. Paul Billheimer wrote a book whose title speaks volumes: "Don't Waste Your Sorrows." We can rebel against them and resist the lessons from them; or we can offer them to the Lord for Him to redeem and bring eternal good from them. Just as such trails can take us to mountain heights in Colorado, these "rocky, rough, barren trails" in life can spiritually take us to heights in Christ.

Amy Carmichael, in her book *Rose From Brier,* relates these truths to an illustration of some rare incense trees from the area of Hazarmaveth (now known as Hadramaut) in Southern Arabia:

> No one could explore this region till lately [circa 1933]. . . .
> Photographs show a blistered land, naked to the sun, cov-

ered for miles with sand, broken stones, or bare rock, almost
waterless, almost treeless.

But one of the high roads of the Old World, the trade route
from India and Persia to Egypt and Syria . . . ran through this
Hazarmaveth, and "it supplied its own fragrant contribution
to that ancient-world commerce." . . . Incense trees grew
along the barren plateaux and in the dry riverbeds.
Merchants came from as far as Persia to find this precious
gum. . . . This substance, universal symbol of prayer, worship, and adoration, was found in such a place. . . .

Sooner or later we find ourselves in some Hazarmaveth of
His appointment. We may miss the incense trees or we may
find them. If we miss them we shall not find them anywhere
else.[1]

To help us not "miss them," identifying these "trees"—the treasures
of these hard times—is important. Throughout Scripture we are exhorted to persevere. Grasping what can be gained from these tough times
can make the difference in our persevering when they come.

One passage in Scripture that clearly addresses this issue is the portion on which this study is based, Hebrews 12:1-3. To begin this chapter, reflect again on these verses:

Therefore, since we are surrounded by such a great cloud
of witnesses, let us throw off everything that hinders and the
sin that so easily entangles, and let us *run with perseverance
the race marked out for us*. Let us fix our eyes on Jesus, the
author and perfecter of our faith, who for the joy set before
him endured the cross, scorning its shame, and sat down at
the right hand of the throne of God. Consider him who
endured such opposition from sinful men, so that you will
not grow weary and lose heart. (Emphasis mine)

Biblical Discovery and Reflection

1. Relating to Amy Carmichael's illustration of the incense trees, how does Scripture address this truth in Isaiah 45:3? Have you been aware of such treasures? Explain.

2. Prior to experiencing a particularly "rough, rocky, barren trail" in my own race, I had been unaware of the "treasures of darkness." I anticipated the path of righteousness being sunny and lined with roses! Therefore, when I first entered this difficult heat of my race, I was surprised by it. I thought if I kept in close relationship with God, His presence would always be real to me. My impression was that this was the experience of all who walked with God. However, as I sought the Lord through Scripture during my confusion and desperation, I discovered that wasn't always so. From Psalm 13:1-2 and 69:1-3, what do you discover that David, the "man after God's own heart," experienced? Does this surprise you?

God's Overall Goal through Perseverance

3. One of the most powerful passages regarding persevering through the darkness and difficult times is James 1:2-4. What is proclaimed as the value of perseverance? What is your response to the deep work the Lord desires to do in us?

God's Power to Redeem

4. What does Paul proclaim God is able to do with whatever touches us in Romans 8:28? With what event in your life does this specifically encourage you, either past or present? Offer this to Him now to redeem. Some ways in which the Lord desires to work things for good are explored below.

God's Good Purposes

(After studying each, identify its purpose by its corresponding number.)

*Purpose 1:*_____

5. One way God can redeem our trials is expressed in 1 Peter 1:3-7. Explain.

    a. Charles Spurgeon, in his devotional *Morning and Evening*, writes:

        Our Lord in His infinite wisdom and superabundant love, sets so high a value on His people's faith that He will not screen them from those trials by which faith is strengthened. You would never have possessed the precious faith that now supports you without the fiery trial of your faith. You are a tree that never would have rooted so well if the wind had not rocked you to and fro, and made you take firm hold on the precious truths of the covenant of grace.[2]

    b. In our Hebrews 12 passage, Jesus is described as "the author and perfecter" of our faith. What does this role of His communicate to you? What do you think are our responsibilities?

        Purpose 2: _____

6. Another way the Lord uses what happens in our lives is revealed in Joseph's experience. Some background: Joseph had been sold to slave traders by his brothers out of their jealousy of him. He was taken to Egypt, where he was sold to Potiphar, one of Pharaoh's officials. Over a long span of time, including many years of unjust imprisonment, Joseph was ultimately honored by Pharaoh and placed in charge of "the whole land of Egypt" (see Gen. 41:41-43). This led to the fulfillment of the dreams God had given Joseph when he was young. When his brothers came to Egypt to buy grain during a time of famine, Joseph was able to provide for his family. What did Joseph proclaim to them in Genesis 45:4-8 and 50:20?

a. Oswald Chambers underscores this truth for our lives in his devotional *My Utmost for His Highest:*

> God gives us a vision, and then He takes us down to the valley to batter us into the shape of that vision. It is in the valley that so many of us give up and faint. Every God-given vision will become real if we will only have patience. . . . God has to take us into the valley and put us through fires and floods to batter us into shape, until we get to the point where He can trust us with the reality of the vision. . . .
>
> . . . Then as sure as God is God and you are you, you will turn out as an exact likeness of the vision. But don't lose heart in the process.[4]

b. How is this truth proclaimed in Ephesians 1:11? How does this encourage you today?

c. Can you give an example of how you have seen God do this, either in your life or in another's?

*Purpose 3:*_____

7. Some of God's highest purposes for us in difficult times are revealed in Hebrews 12:10-11. What does God desire for us? What quality guides His discipline in this higher purpose?

a. Jerry Bridges, in *Trusting God,* also addresses this passage and these truths:

> The good that God works for in our lives is conformity to the likeness of His Son. It is not necessarily comfort or happiness but conformity to Christ in ever-increasing measure in this life and in its fullness in eternity.
>
> We see this . . . in Hebrews 12:10. . . . To share in God's holiness is an equivalent expression to being conformed to the likeness of Christ. God knows exactly what he intends we become and he knows exactly what circumstances, both

good and bad, are necessary to produce that result in our
lives. . . .

The author of Hebrews readily admits that discipline is
painful [9:11]. But he also assures us it is profitable. . . . The
purpose of God's discipline is not to punish us but to transform us.[5]

b. What confidence did Job have regarding this, as expressed in
   Job 23:10?

c. How have you seen a fiery trial refine you?

*Purpose 4:*_____

8. As we become more like Christ, God's ultimate goal in our relation-
    ship with Him is accomplished: Oneness with Himself (review
    John 17:20-23, 26). Oswald Chambers states: "From Jesus Christ's
    perspective, oneness with Him, with nothing between, is the only
    good thing."[6] How does God's refining deepen this oneness?

*Purpose 5:*_____

9. What are some other results of refining, gleaned from Jesus' words in
   John 15, explored below?

   a. What results will we experience, according to verses 1-5?

   b. What will God receive through our lives, expressed in verse 8?

   c. What will we experience more fully? See verse 11.

   d. How will our prayer life be affected according to verses 7 and
       16 (see also James 5:16-18)?

*Purpose 6:*_____

10. Oswald Chambers, in *God's Workmanship*, adds another great value and important dimension to our suffering and the importance of persevering:

> We suffer, and God alone knows why. . . . Neither is it at all satisfying to say that suffering develops character. There was more in Job's suffering that was required to develop his character, and so it is with the sanctified soul. The preface to Job's story lets in the light from the revelation point of view, namely, that God's honor was at stake, and the issue fought out in this man's soul vindicated God's honor.[8]

a. Philip Yancey echoes this as he reflects on Job's experience. He writes: "The opening and closing chapters of Job prove that God was greatly affected by the response of one man and that cosmic issues were at stake. . . . The Wager [between God and Satan] resolved decisively that the faith of a single human being counts for very much indeed."[9]

b. How does it impact you that "cosmic issues" are at stake in your trial?

Personal Application and Response

11. Review the good purposes of God examined in the lesson thus far. List those here. (Add any others you can think of.)

12. How does understanding the good that the Lord can bring out of difficulty help you? How can focusing on the goals attained through perseverance enable you to persevere? Be specific for yourself.

13. How have you seen the Lord use difficulty in the past to accomplish His good purposes in you? Give examples.

14. What are you currently experiencing that is challenging you to persevere? Record those here.

    a. As you are faced with choices in how you will respond in each situation you listed, do you find yourself currently rebelling against God's purposes or yielding to Him for them to be accomplished?

    b. Do you struggle with not valuing His good purposes? Process your feelings with Him. He does know, and He cares. What, if anything, is more important to you?

15. Which "treasures of darkness" do you long for (or would you like Him to give you the desire for)? Express your heart to the Lord in this.

16. Watchman Nee encourages us to persevere in his book *The Normal Christian Life* by explaining what we will experience when the time of darkness is over. He shares from his experience:

    > The Lord graciously laid me aside once . . . and put me, spiritually, into utter darkness. It was almost as though he had forsaken me. . . . But remember, there must be a full night . . . in darkness. It cannot be hurried; he knows what he is doing.
    > . . . It will seem as though nothing is happening. . . . Lie quiet. All is in darkness, but it is only for a night. . . . Afterwards you will find that everything is given back to you in glorious resurrection; and nothing can measure the difference between what was before and what now is![10]

    a. Once in my "dark night," the Lord sent an older, godly woman to encourage me. After hearing me share regarding my present difficult time, she took my face in her hands, looked me right in the eyes, and exhorted me, "Don't give up!" She assured me God would fulfill His purposes for me and concluded by saying, in essence, "It will all be worth it!" Many times during my journey I have hung on to her words. Now I pass them on to you as well.

b.   After the difficulty was over, when "morning" had come, I found her words and Nee's to be true! I did know Christ better, was stronger in my faith, and was experiencing more of His resurrection power in my living and speaking. *He* did it! He worked quietly in His grace—and faithfully accomplished His purposes. Truly, I proclaim as well, "It was all worth it! *Christ is worth it!* And God is faithful!"

17.   Give each difficulty you recorded in question 15 to Him to redeem. Ask Him to accomplish His good purposes in you, explored in this lesson. Yield to Him; and trust Him!

18.   In closing, write out James 1:2-4. Personalize this, making it your prayer.

Group Discussion Questions

1. What dynamics tend to keep us more focused on our circumstances rather than on God's purposes in our circumstances? How can we shift our focus to be fixed more on Him and His higher purposes? How can our values become more aligned with the Lord's?

2. Do you believe that God is able to fulfill His purposes through a specific trial? Why or why not? How would your belief influence your willingness to yield to Him in it? (We will explore our role in this in the next chapter.)

3. Which higher purposes of God's have you personally seen Him accomplish in your life through the difficulties you have experienced?

4. Do you believe that "cosmic issues" and eternal matters are actually at stake in your trial? How would this truth influence your desire to persevere and allow God to accomplish His purposes through it? What difference does this make to you today?

5. Which of God's good purposes explored in this lesson especially stirs your heart for your own life? Spend time praying for His purposes to be accomplished through your present circumstances.

❧ 10 ❧

Persevering When the Race Gets Tough
Part Two: Discovering How *to Persevere*

When my sister discovered she had breast cancer, her race suddenly took a turn for the worse. The terrain became rocky, skies grew dark, and the course seemed interminably long. "When I was in treatment," she wrote regarding this time, "I needed to see the light at the end of the tunnel—the date when I would have my last chemo. Several delays due to infection and low blood counts meant they had to keep moving that date further out. I felt like a baseball player rounding third base and heading for home, but someone kept moving the plate farther and farther away. I kept running, but it didn't seem like I was getting there."

Perhaps you have felt this way at times in your race. There can be difficult times that seem to never end. We can become discouraged, feeling that the Lord deserted us. At times, we may be tempted to give up—to drop out of the race, go sit on the sidelines in despair. Even though we may understand the values of our trials, just as my sister understood the value of the chemotherapy, we may still feel it's too much, and we can't endure it.

In my personal journey of faith, I experienced such a time, which I referenced in the previous chapter. Out of that time came the understanding of these values of difficulty and darkness, as well as seeing the Lord do a deep work in me. In addition, when the going got rough and God seemed not to be there, He taught me a lot about *how* to keep going, keep persevering in the race, even when I didn't feel like it.

The passage in Scripture that once again gives us insight into how to persevere is the portion on which this study is based, Hebrews 12:1-3. To begin this chapter, review these verses as rendered in *The Message:*

> Do you see what this means—all these pioneers who blazed the way, all these veterans cheering us on? It means we'd better get on with it. Strip down, start running—and never quit! No extra spiritual fat, no parasitic sins. Keep your eyes on *Jesus,* who both began and finished this race we're in. Study how he did it. Because he never lost sight of where he was headed—that exhilarating finish in and with God—he could put up with anything along the way: cross, shame, whatever. And now he's *there,* in the place of honor, right alongside God. When you find yourselves flagging in your faith, go over that story again, item by item, that long litany of hostility he plowed through. *That* will shoot adrenaline into your souls![1]

Biblical Discovery and Reflection

1. When we feel "worn down" or "beaten down," what encouragement are we given in Isaiah 42:3?

2. In Scripture we are given many examples of those who have gone before us who have endured lengthy and difficult trials (such as Joseph, Job, and Jeremiah). Yet, who is not only our greatest *example* in perseverance but also our *source* of endurance, discerned from our Hebrews passage above as well as 2 Thessalonians 3:5?

    a. Sheila Walsh, in *Life Is Tough but God Is Faithful,* succinctly states: "The truth is, ultimately none of us will be able to stand unless we daily throw ourselves into the saving arms of God. We can't do it on our own. It's not about us. We have no strength apart from Him."[2]

b. How does it help you today to realize it's not up to you to muster the strength to make it—that there is a Source of strength and endurance that far surpasses your own?

c. In 1 Thessalonians 5:23-24, what encouragement are we given by Paul (who had to greatly persevere)?

3. In *The Sacred Romance*, the authors give us further insight into how we can persevere by considering how Jesus persevered. They ask,

> How did Jesus sustain his passionate heart in the face of brutal opposition? *He never lost sight of where he was headed.* . . . He remembered both where he had come from and where he was going (John 13:3.) And so must we. . . .
> . . . Jesus is called the "author and perfecter of our faith" (12:2). He is the One who put the romance in our hearts and the One who first opened our eyes to see that our deepest desire is fulfilled in him. He started us on the journey and he has bound himself to see us through.[3]

Underscore the specific points that help us persevere.

4. Jeremiah's life reveals some secrets to persevering as well. Eugene Peterson, in *Run with the Horses*, writes:

> Jeremiah did not resolve to stick it out for twenty-three years, no matter what; he got up every morning with the sun. The day was God's day, not the people's. He didn't get up to face rejection, he got up to meet with God. . . . That is the secret of his persevering pilgrimage. . . .
> Where did Jeremiah learn his persistence? . . . He learned it from God.
> Jeremiah learned to live persistently toward God because God lived persistently toward him. . . . At the very center of this dark time . . . there is this verse: "The steadfast love of the

LORD never ceases, his mercies never come to an end; they are new every morning; great is thy faithfulness" (Lam. 3:22-23). . . .

That is the source of Jeremiah's living persistence. . . . He was up before the sun, listening to God's word. Rising early, he was quiet and attentive before his Lord. . . .

Jeremiah had a defined priority: persistently rising early, he listened to God, then spoke and acted what he heard.[4]

Highlight the phrases that encourage you as well as those that reveal Jeremiah's secrets in persevering.

5. Another secret of perseverance illustrated by Jeremiah is that he took one day at a time. A hiker, Henry Shires, learned this lesson that relates to our journey as well. Walking 2,658 miles in 130 days, he completed his goal to walk the Pacific Crest National Scenic Trail, connecting Mexico to Canada. This trail "passes from searing heat to summer snow, encompassing most of the life zones in North America. This year, more than 200 people attempted to walk the entire trail: two-thirds failed to complete it."[5] What was Henry's secret? It is revealed in the title of his article, "One Step at a Time"! (Henry was inspired in this concept by Justice Sandra Day O'Connor's commencement address when he graduated from Colorado College. The title of her address was "One Step at a Time—And Keep Walking.")

    a. Why is that an important lesson for us in our journey as well? How can we do this and not dwell on how long our challenging journey might be?

    b. Mr. Shires also stated that although such a hike was a physical challenge, he feels the body's part was actually only 10 percent of the battle. He comments, "It's the brain that wins or loses the war." He continues to reflect: "The person who left Mexico is not the same one who entered Canada. I am forever changed by this experience, some ways apparent to others, other ways known only to me."[6] What parallels do you see from his experience to our journey?

6. As we take one day at a time and spend time daily with the Lord, what helps us draw on Christ's strength and endurance? Consider both Proverbs 4:20-22 and Ephesians 3:16-17, along with Hebrews 4:14-16.

    a. What is ours to do?

    b. Why must we actively draw on Christ's life?

7. Another action we are to take is identified in Ephesians 6:18.

    a. Rather than feeling we're doing nothing, how can prayer enable us to persevere? For example, consider how important it is to join our hearts with His in praying for His purposes to be accomplished.

    b. How can the prayers of others, perhaps when we feel we cannot even pray ourselves, strengthen and sustain us? Can you give an example?

    (1) During my sister's battle with breast cancer, she reflected, "When I was first diagnosed I felt so alone. I was in a dark closet battling something I couldn't see that was so close yet so strangely elusive. But my family, friends, coworkers all rallied around me. I discovered that people around the country were praying for me, people I didn't even know. Their prayers strengthened me. We were a team, and that team included the best medical care available."
    In the year following her battle, she walked in Denver's "Race for the Cure." Her experience there illustrated this support. She writes: "As I walked that day, I found I was part of an even bigger team. It was like a reunion with a family I

didn't know I had. . . As I walked, my hips and back began to ache and my feet hurt. I was reminded of the times during my battle that had not been pleasant, but I drew on my faith and the support of my team and found the strength to deal with it. . . . On that cool October morning in Denver, I kept walking, but every time I turned a corner and thought I'd see the finish line, it wasn't there. I needed to keep going. People standing on the curbs handed me cups of water as I passed by. Their outstretched hands were like the words of encouragement and hugs I received throughout my treatment, each one giving me added strength."

(2) Who would you like to ask to pray for you? Record their names, checking each off as you contact them for prayer.

(3) As we go throughout our days, let's be aware of those around us who need a hug or a drink of "living water." Let us be a source of encouragement to others to persevere in their race—for their sake and God's. Is there anyone who comes to mind at this time who may need a phone call or a note of encouragement?

8. Another important dimension in persevering is revealed in this Ephesians 6:10-18 passage along with 1 Peter 5:8-10.

    a. It's important to understand the battle being waged against us. What do you discover?

    b. This battle is perhaps most intense during our "dark night," or time of difficulty. What are some tactics the Enemy uses to discourage and defeat us during a difficult heat in our race? Which ones does he specifically use in your life?

    c. In Ephesians 6:13-18, what provisions are we given for this battle, and what are we instructed to do? Record these below, along with how applying each helps us persevere.

d. What are we clearly and strongly exhorted to do, summing it all up, in Ephesians 6:10?

e. At the end of this time, what will the Lord do, according to 1 Peter 5:10?

9. What advice are we given in our Hebrews 12:1-3 passage as to whom we are to "fix our eyes on"? (This will be explored in depth in chapter 11.)

a. In addition to being helped by Christ Himself and encouraged by His example of perseverance, why would it be critical to hang on to the truths of His character when our feelings might mislead us into being deceived regarding who He is?

b. What specific truths regarding the character of God are helpful for you to hold on to? (Consider, for example, the truth proclaimed in Isaiah 43:1-2 and Hebrews 13:5.)

c. One significant insight for me regarding a truth of God's character during my "dark night" came from Jesus' experience on the cross. Jesus knew the Father totally. They were one. At Jesus' lowest, darkest point—when He was being crucified and was actually forsaken (on our behalf so that we never will be forsaken)—He proclaimed in a loud voice, "Father, into your hands I commit my spirit" (Luke 23:46). For Jesus to know He could do this in His darkest moment speaks volumes to me. If there was any reason why the Father couldn't be completely trusted at all times, Jesus would not have been able to do this at His point of death. This says to me that, even when I don't understand and all may be dark, I can commit myself to God and trust Him.

d. Sheila Walsh reveals a truth that sustained her in her "dark night": "As we began to uncover some painful issues, I felt as if my heart was being ripped out of my body, but I still knew that Jesus loved me. We have this fact to hold onto in the darkest nights of our lives. It will never change. It will always be true. Yes, Jesus loves me!"[7] (See Romans 8:38-39.) Hold on to this reality!

    e.   Do you struggle with any questions regarding God's character? Record those here.

10.   An important dimension to persevering is discovered in Luke 11:5-13. What does Jesus exhort us to do here, and what does He promise?

11.   Because of who Christ is, even when "in darkness," what are we exhorted to do in Isaiah 50:10 (see also Ps. 62:8)?

    a.   Why can we trust, according to Psalm 9:10?

    b.   As we trust, what will result, according to Isaiah 26:3-4?

12.   Finally, enabling us to persevere through the darkness and intensity of trial is God's grace. When my "dark night" was over, I realized the Lord had been there all along and that He held on to me when I was too weary to hold on to Him. His grace, mercy, and sustaining Presence got me through.

    a.   Consider the following verse of the great hymn "Amazing Grace":

    Through many dangers, toils and snares, I have already come;
    Tis grace has brought me safe thus far, and grace will lead me home.[8]

    b.   Anne Graham Lotz, in her book *Just Give Me Jesus*, addresses these truths. In writing of the Holy Spirit as our "comforter," she explains that the Greek word is *parakletos*, "which literally means one called alongside to help." She relates the story of an event in the 1996 Olympics, when one of the runners in the 440-meter race pulled a hamstring. She records then what happened next.

As the crowd stood, holding its collective breath, a man ran out of the stands to the young athlete. It was his father! As the television crew relayed the moving scene to the watching world, the microphones picked up the runner's words: "Dad, you've got to help me across the finish line. I've trained all my life for this race." And so the father put his arm around his son, and together, they limped across the finish line to a standing ovation!

In the race of life, God our heavenly Father has come alongside us through the Person of the Holy Spirit. And
    when we think we can't go one more step,
    when the race becomes painful beyond endurance,
    when our hearts feel heavy,
    when our minds become dull,
    when our spirits are burned out,
we have the *Parakletos*, Who comes alongside us, puts His everlasting arms around us, and gently walks with us to the finish. The applause you hear is from "the great cloud of witnesses" who rejoice in your victory![9]

c. Thank the Lord for His sustaining Presence and His grace, and cast yourself upon Him. Be assured that He, as your *Parakletos,* has His arms around you and faithfully supports you.

Personal Application and Response

13. What situation(s), if any, are you being called to persevere in at this time? Pour out your heart to the Lord regarding your struggles in this

and the pain you are experiencing. Seek His direction if there is anything specific He would have you do.

14. What tactics of the Enemy are you battling? How can you specifically counter them?

15. No matter how dark your night gets, or how rough your race becomes, what truths of God's character will you hang on to?

16. In review, when going through difficult times, take the following steps:

    a. *Ask for discernment* regarding God's purposes in your trial. Are you to stand against the Enemy and this is not to touch you at all? Or is God allowing this to touch you for His greater and higher purposes?

    b. *Seek direction* regarding any specific steps the Lord would have you take in your circumstances. Then obey, knowing He goes with you and has gone before you.

    c. *Bind Satan* in the power, authority, and name of Jesus. *Stand against* his purposes and tactics in your life.

    d. *Yield yourself* to the Lord for His good purposes. Don't resist His work in you.

    e. *Pray for God's good purposes to be accomplished by His Spirit.* Be proactive!

    f. *Ask the Lord to lead you into truth* regarding your specific doubts or questions. Ask Him to reveal Himself to you in deeper ways, so that you would know Him better. Keep seeking!

    g. *Stay in His Word!* Spend time daily with Him, regardless of any apparent benefit.

h. *Keep your eyes fixed on Jesus!* Focus on what you know to be true regarding His character. Do not let feelings determine your faith. Resist the temptation to look ahead. Simply take "one day at a time."

i. *Pray that He would be glorified* in you and through you because of this time. Remember, His honor is at stake!

j. *Cast yourself upon Him and His grace,* asking Him to impart to you His strength and endurance so you would persevere and finish well.

k. *Ask friends to pray for you,* and with you, when possible.

l. *Trust Him!*

17. As you take these above steps, the Lord *will* accomplish His purposes! Often, it is a mystery how He does it, because His working is seldom apparent—but somehow, by His Spirit, He does it. For documentation, read 1 Thessalonians 5:23-24.

18. Express your heart to the Lord now regarding the difficulties you are experiencing.

19. In conclusion, personalize the encouragement given regarding perseverance in James 5:10-11.

Group Discussion Questions

1. What are common questions we struggle with in our faith during difficult times? What choices do we have when doubts arise? What has been your experience in dealing with your questions?

2. What tactics does the Enemy use to discourage us in times of trial, to keep us from persevering? What does he use most commonly in your life? How can you counteract these tactics? Be specific.

3. In your own "battles" and through your difficult times, what has helped you the most in your faith? What steps have you found particularly helpful in persevering? What additional insights did you receive from this lesson?

4. How have you seen the importance of the support of other believers when going through difficult times? Why do we sometimes resist asking others to pray?

5. What have you personally discovered about the Lord Himself through your trials?

❧ 11 ❧

Fixing Our Eyes on Jesus

The secret to running our race well is this: Fixing our eyes on Jesus! Not only is this the key for persevering, but it provides our motivation for all dimensions of the race. He is our treasure! He is our gold! Everything else pales in comparison to knowing Him increasingly in this life, hearing His "well done" when we enter His presence, and enjoying a love relationship with Him now and for eternity. To run our best, to give our all to the race, we must keep our eyes fixed on Jesus.

Jesus ran well because He had His eyes fixed on *us!* As explored previously, we are His gold! In addition to being restored to His Father, to have a love relationship with us was His motivation and His goal, and nothing could deter Him. No matter what He faced, regardless of other appeals that tantalized, He determinedly marched toward the cross for this "joy that was set before Him" (Heb. 12:1-3). Therefore, the author of Hebrews exhorts us to run toward Him in this same manner.

To explore further this secret of fixing our eyes on Jesus—what this means and how we do this—turn now to God's Word.

Biblical Discovery and Reflection

1. In any task, what can happen when we lose sight of our goal? Can you give an example?

2. How does Matthew 25:1-10 picture those who chose to persevere and those who chose not to?

a. Why did some drop out of the race? Relate this to life today in our race.

b. How do you think the others kept motivated not to give up in their race (not let their oil run out)?

c. Where do you see yourself in this parable? What, if anything, tempts you to let your oil run out and head in another direction? What keeps you motivated to keep your lamp full and run your best to the end?

3. As seen from Hebrews 12:1-3, to persevere in our faith, we are strongly exhorted to fix our eyes on Jesus! How is this key endorsed in Moses' experience, according to Hebrews 11:24-27?

4. This essential action is also endorsed by Jehoshaphat in 2 Chronicles 20. When his battle was intense and his circumstances were overwhelming, where were his eyes? Read 2 Chronicles 20:2-12.

a. What encouragement was Jehoshaphat given in verse 15? Write these words out here, personalizing them. (To underscore God's power over the Enemy, see Luke 10:19; Ephesians 6:10; and 1 John 4:4.)

b. What truth was Jehoshaphat given as the basis not to fear? See 2 Chronicles 20:17. Apply this truth to you for your circumstances as well (see also Isa. 43:2; Rom. 8:38-39; Heb. 13:5).

c. How can focusing on these two truths help free you from fear as well?

d. As we keep our eyes on Him, what are we able to do in spite of our circumstances, just as the people did in Jehoshaphat's day? See 2 Chronicles 20:21. Will you choose to do this now?

5. *Praise* is not only a wonderful response to who God is, but it is also a powerful tool in helping us keep our eyes fixed on Him. What does David say he does at all times in Psalm 34:1? What lesson is here for us?

6. *God's Word* helps us stay focused on the Lord and inspires us to praise. (For example, read Psalm 145.) How has Scripture helped you keep your eyes on Jesus? Can you give a specific example?

7. In times of difficulty, what can occur if we take our eyes off of Jesus? What does Peter's experience illustrate in Matthew 14:22-31?

   a. For me, looking at circumstances will invariably cause me to sink! In fact, a friend of mine years ago was sharing her tendency to do this as well. She said that when she is fearful or anxious, she asks herself this question: "Where are my eyes?" Inevitably, she said, they are on herself, a threatening person, or difficult circumstances. When she gets them back on the Lord, then she has peace. Now every time I become anxious, I ask myself, "Where are my eyes?"

   b. As we focus on Him, what else is nurtured, discerned from Jesus' words to Peter in verse 31 of the Matthew passage above? Explain.

8. In this situation, Jesus called Peter to come to Him. As Peter kept his eyes on Jesus, he wasn't afraid. We, too, are called by Jesus to come to Him, to get to know Him, to walk with Him—in all circumstances. How can this be frightening for some people? Do you experience any fears regarding growing closer to Christ? Talk with Him about these. How can keeping your eyes on Him free you from those fears?

9. In addition to the fears already considered, what fears can we have in serving the Lord, using our gifts for the sake of His kingdom? How does it help us in overcoming these fears to focus on Jesus?

    a. Moses had fear when the Lord called him. Read of his experience in Exodus 3:4-14.

        (1) Who was Moses focusing on when he felt afraid?

        (2) In essence, whom did the Lord tell Moses to focus on instead? Why would that free Moses from fear? Explain.

    b. For me, when opportunities first came to speak, I felt very much like Moses—I was extremely fearful! My mouth got dry, my neck became blotchy, my heart pounded. But because I felt the Lord was asking me to proclaim Him, I did so out of obedience. The only thing I found that helped me was to fix my eyes on Jesus. I had to get my eyes off of myself and my inadequacies, along with my fear of what others would think of me, and turn my eyes on *Him!* I focused on His faithfulness as well as wanting to glorify Him, because I loved Him and because He is worthy. As I maintained that focus, my fear was conquered. At times, I didn't do as well as I would have liked, but that helped free me from caring so much what others thought. Jesus faithfully used those times in my life to do an important work. Fixing my eyes on Him helped me to not count the cost, because He was worth it all.

    c. Does fear hold you back to any degree in serving Him? To be freed from fear, what qualities of His will you focus on?

10. Keeping our eyes on Jesus frees us from the bondage of pleasing others. How does Mary (Martha's sister) illustrate this? Read Matthew 26:6-13. (Mary is identified as this woman in John 12:1-3.)

a. One of the biggest snares for us in our race is caring what others think. We can be running our race, but our eyes are on the crowd in the stands to see if they're cheering rather than on our goal. To what degree do you struggle with this?

b. Why did their criticism not matter to Mary? Where were her eyes? What was her heart?

c. What commendation did Jesus give Mary? How does this encourage us in our race?

Personal Application and Response

11. How much of a distraction is pleasing others for you? Are your eyes more on people than on Jesus? Are you running to gain the applause of the crowd primarily, or the commendation of Jesus first and foremost?

a. Gail MacDonald, in her book *High Call, High Privilege*, shares her discoveries in this arena.

> Serving people in the name of Jesus is a joy, even fun. But worrying about who I am pleasing can be a curse. It was time for me to be sure that I knew the difference. . . . A string of words entered my life and brought a new focus to my spiritual perspective: *Live as if you are playing to an audience of One.*
> I'd often heard Gordon talk about athletes who wisely ignore the crowd and "play it to the coach." In my case, the coach was Jesus. . . .
> I've met more than a few women who are living for multiple audiences, striving frantically to hear the applause of each one of them. . . .

. . . What has come to me is that the more I've focused on playing all of life to Jesus, what characterizes him, what pleases him, what points others to him, the more these other issues have found their proper place.[2]

b. Some helpful tips in keeping your eyes on Jesus, to seek after Him and live for Him, are:

(1) Write your life goals out and keep them where you will see them daily. (For my computer's screen saver, I have in bold letters: "Go for the Gold!" Then the verse references follow, "Philippians 3:10-14" and "Ephesians 3:16-21.") What are your goals and desires? Where will you post these to help keep you focused?

(2) Pray for these goals to be accomplished. Each day we pray for that which is important to us, such as our families and our concerns. Let's incorporate our desires in Christ into our daily prayers as well.

(3) What other steps can you take to help keep you focused on Christ rather than what others think?

12. *What we fix our eyes on is important because that will determine what our lives will be about!*

a. We began this study by considering all that pretends to be "gold" in our life. In chapter 1, question 15, review those things that appealed to you to run after. Having nearly completed this study, do they now still have the same appeal? What do you discover?

b. Why is living for Jesus and growing in Him of greatest value, discerned from 2 Corinthians 4:17-18? Write out this passage and post this where you will see it daily.

13. *Also what we fix our eyes (and mind) on is important because it will determine our peace.* Review Isaiah 26:3-4. How have you experienced this reality?

14. As we keep our eyes fixed on Jesus what occurs within us? Review 2 Corinthians 3:18.

    a. A. W. Tozer "calls us to see that real world of the spiritual that lies beyond the physical world that so ensnares us. He begs us to please God and forget the crowd. He implores us to worship God that we might become more like Him."[3]

    b. In Hebrews 12, the Greek word for fix is *"aphorao,* which means to direct our gaze on Him and to turn it away from everything else."[4] Take time now to turn from all else to behold Him alone and worship Him.

15. As we keep our eyes fixed on Him, we not only benefit, but He is delighted! As the king praised the maiden in Song of Songs for having doves' eyes (1:15; 4:1), so Jesus praises us. Watchman Nee provides insight for us regarding this: "The eyes of the dove can only see one thing at a time, and this signifies singleness of purpose. . . . Her heart is only and wholly for the Beloved. It is this which makes her so fair in His eyes, therefore the King praises her."[5]

    a. In contemplating this delight of lovers, read His words to you as expressed in Song of Songs 4:9-15. What are your responses?

    b. Do you desire to delight His heart? If so, keep your eyes fixed on Him. Also, as we do so, we grow to love Him more fully and desire Him more completely. Our heart longs to become more fully pleasing to Him and to live totally for Him. Express your heart to Him here.

16. In closing, in keeping with the analogy of Jesus as our Bridegroom and we as His bride, reflect on the wedding itself. As the bride progresses down the aisle, where are her eyes fixed? Where are the groom's eyes focused? Apply this to how you are moving through life, increasingly coming closer to Christ. Savor this image each day for yourself! In truth, this is the love relationship you are called to first and foremost in Him. Daily, keep your eyes fixed on your Bridegroom!

Group Discussion Questions

1. As we go through our days with our eyes fixed on Jesus, does that mean we are oblivious to everything else around us? Do we ignore practical matters or business issues? Are we so fixed on the spiritual and eternal that we can't relate to others enmeshed in this world? How does this work, practically speaking, to have our eyes fixed on Jesus yet very aware of, and involved with, all around us as we go through our days? Explain.

2. What things commonly distract our focus from Christ and disrupt our race in Him and toward Him? How can these deterrents and temptations be overcome? Share examples where possible.

3. What things most commonly discourage you in your faith and draw your focus off of Christ? How can you resist that temptation?

4. What helps you keep your eyes fixed on Jesus? What results have you experienced?

5. How does the love relationship of the bride and Bridegroom help and inspire you?

❧ 1 2 ❧

Crossing the Finish Line!

One day, we each will cross the finish line! That's a given. Exactly when is what we don't know. This final finish line occurs either when we go to be with our Lord or when He returns at the end of time. What will crossing this finish line be like? In this closing chapter, let's explore this joy awaiting us.

In addition to our final finish line, each leg of the race has its own completion. Each season we are in, each trial we endure, has its own finish line. How important to cross each finish line well, hear the cheers surrounding us, and receive our Lord's praise. Having this perspective also helps us persevere!

To examine both dimensions, let's turn to God's Word.

Biblical Discovery and Reflection

1. What mixture of feelings can people experience as they think about crossing that final finish line? What do you personally feel?

2. Each of us is aware of our own mortality. At some point, life as we know it will end. Yet what assurance are we given in Romans 8:35-39 that helps alleviate fear?

3. What happens to us spiritually at the time of death? What does Jesus reveal through His words on the cross to the thief being

crucified next to Him? See Luke 23:39-43. What hope does this give you?

a. What convictions did the Apostle Paul have regarding what happens at the time of physical death? Read 2 Corinthians 5:1-9 and Philippians 1:20-24.

b. Dwight Moody stated his assurance on one occasion: "Some day you will read in the papers that D. L. Moody of East Northfield is dead. Don't you believe one word of it! At that moment I shall be more alive than I am now."[1] How exciting!

c. Here are some supportive experiences:

(1) When my mother was dying, I was at her side. However, she slipped into a coma and the doctors said she might remain in that state for some time. After a week, my husband and I decided to drive back home, a trip of several days. Throughout the return trip, we kept in touch with the hospital, with always the same report: "condition unchanged." However, about two hours outside of our home town (Colorado Springs), a surge of joy suddenly filled my spirit and the words burned in my mind, "Set free!" Sharing what happened with my husband, I reflected, "I wonder if Mom just died." Calling the hospital, I discovered she did die at that time! How very special: "Joy!" "Set free!" That was exactly what my mom was experiencing!

(2) Billy Graham relates the experience of Joseph Everett. "When Joseph Everett was dying, he said, 'Glory! Glory! Glory!' and he continued exclaiming glory for over twenty-five minutes."[2] How does this impact you?

d. What are your conclusions regarding what occurs at the time

Fix Your Eyes on Jesus

of passing from this life to the next? Do these examples change your view of death at all? What feelings do you now have regarding that experience?

4. In our lifetime, we may experience something new. We may not experience death. What does Jesus say will occur one day in John 14:1-3 (see also Matt. 24:30-31; Acts 1:6-11)?

    a. In the wedding tradition of Jesus' day, the words that Jesus states in John 14 are the prescribed words a bridegroom says to his fiancée before returning to his parents' home. After preparing a home for his bride, the bridegroom returns for her. The wedding is then performed, and he takes her back to the home he has prepared. Jesus often referred to Himself as the Bridegroom (for example, see Matt. 9:14-15; 25:1-13). How does it impact you to realize these very words were a part of the wedding tradition of that day?

    b. In Revelation 19:6-9, what will occur at the end of time, underscoring Jesus' words?

        (1) Are you absolutely certain you will be with Him after your life here on earth? Will you be participating in the wedding supper of the Lamb? What invitation are you given in Revelation 22:17? What is your response? Express this to Him now.

        (2) How does realizing that you are His bride, and that there will be a wedding celebration, motivate you to want to be ready? What do you think being ready involves?

    c. A. W. Tozer writes:

        We live between two mighty events—that of His incarnation, death and resurrection, and that of His ultimate appearing and the glorification of those He died to save. This is the interim time for the saints—but it is not a vacuum. He has given us much to do and He asks for our faithfulness. . . .

. . . Looking back to His grace and love; looking forward to His coming and glory; meanwhile actively working and joyously hoping—until He comes![3]

d. What responsibility do you think we have in helping others be ready—preparing the body of Christ to be His bride? How does your love for Christ motivate you to participate in this?

5. What will be the response of all people when Christ returns, revealed in Philippians 2:9-11? How does knowing that all will one day recognize Jesus as Lord and King help us endure any persecution we may experience now? What excitement does it impart to know also that Jesus will receive the glory and worship due Him?

6. What will happen for all who belong to Jesus, according to 1 Corinthians 15:49-57?

In celebration, write out the expression of victory in verse 57.

7. Other wonderful truths of what awaits us are revealed in Revelation 21:1-6. What else will be made new? (For thrilling descriptions of what this will be like, read Rev. 21:22–22:6.)

a. Support for the wholeness we receive is related by Billy Graham, when he wrote of his grandmother's deathbed experience. Billy's grandfather, Ben, died before his grandmother. Dr. Graham notes that during the battle of Gettysburg, Ben had lost both a leg and an eye. When Billy's grandmother was dying, he records her experience:

"My grandmother sat up in her bed, smiled, and said, 'I see Jesus and His hand outstretched to me. And there is Ben, and he has both of his eyes and both of his legs.'[4] What are your responses to her experience?

b. From the Revelation 21:1-6 passage above, what will "be no more"?

c. What will Jesus do for us? Stop and reflect on this for all those tears you have cried.

d. How do these truths encourage you today?

8. In anticipation of all that awaits her, Joni Eareckson Tada, confined to her wheelchair, writes the following:

> Though I spend my mortal lifetime in this chair,
> I refuse to waste it living in despair.
> And though others may receive
> Gifts of healing, I believe
> That He has given me a gift beyond compare. . . .
>
> For heaven is nearer to me,
> And at times it is all I can see.
> Secret music I hear
> Coming down to my ear;
> And I know it is playing for me.
>
> For I am Christ the Savior's own bride,
> And redeemed I shall stand by His side.
> He will say, "Shall we dance?"
> And our endless romance
> Will be worth all the tears I have cried.[5]

She also writes:

> I was reminded that in heaven I will be free to jump up,
> dance, kick, and do aerobics. And although I'm sure Jesus
> will be delighted to watch me rise on tiptoe, there's some-
> thing I plan to do that may please Him more. If possible,
> somewhere, sometime before the party gets going, some-
> time before the guests are called to the banquet table at
> the Wedding Feast of the Lamb, the first thing I plan to do
> on resurrected legs is to drop on grateful, glorified knees.
> I will quietly kneel at the feet of Jesus. . . .
>
> And after a while, I shall spring to my feet, stretch my
> arms, and shout out to anyone within earshot of the whole
> universe, "Worthy is the Lamb who was slain to receive
> power and riches, wisdom and might, honor and glory
> and blessing"![6]

How do her words—how does her heart—impact you? What
   encouragement do you receive for your present circumstances?

9.   What incredible revelation does Jesus give in Luke 12:35-37
     regarding what *He* will do for *us* at this banquet? What is your
     response as you consider Jesus doing this for *you?*

10. What will we receive for how we have lived, according to Jesus'
     words in Revelation 22:12?

     a.   Jesus discloses this truth in His parable recorded in Luke
          19:11-27. What do you discover (see also Matt. 16:27; 1 Cor.
          3:8; Rev. 11:18)?

     b.   Joni comments regarding Luke's parable and these truths:

          > I love serving God. And if we've been faithful in earthly
          > service, our responsibility in heaven will increase propor-
          > tionately. No, I take that back. It won't be increased in

proportion. God's too generous for that. Our service will increase completely out of proportion. It doesn't take a rocket scientist to read the formula Jesus gives in His heaven parable in Luke 19:17: "Well done, my good servant!" his master replied. "Because you have been trustworthy in a very small matter, take charge of ten cities."

. . . Those who are faithful in a few minor things will be put in charge over multitudinous things.

. . . The more faithful you are in this life, the more responsibility you will be given in the life to come.

Please note Jesus doesn't say, "Because you've been successful in a very small matter," He says, "Because you've been trustworthy.". . . Success isn't the key. Faithfulness is. Being bigger and better is not the point. It's being obedient.

The more trustworthy you've been, the greater your service in eternity.[7]

Referring to Revelation 3:21, Joni writes:

> We will sit with Christ on His throne and reign with Him. We will be given a sphere of authority and oversight of God's eternal kingdom.
>
> We get to reign with Him, plus more.
>
> . . . Romans 8:17 elevates us to an incredible position [as heirs]. . . . We will join Him in overseeing His and our inheritance. . . .
>
> We get to reign on earth with Christ![8] (see also Rev. 22:5)

What is your response to these realities?

    c.   Charles Spurgeon, in his book *The Second Coming of Christ,* also documents this:

Remember how the Lord will say, *"Well done, thou good and faithful servant: thou hast been faithful over a few things, I will make thee ruler over many things"* (Matthew 25:21). The servant is to keep on doing something, you see. Instead of having some little bit of a village to govern, he is to be made ruler over some great province. . . .

Reading further in Luke, we find: *"Of a truth I say unto you, that he will make him ruler over all that he hath"* (Luke 12:44). That is, the man who has been a faithful and wise steward of God here will be called of God to more eminent service hereafter. If a person serves his Master well, when his Master comes, He will promote him to still higher service.[9]

d. Billy Graham remarks: "I think that when we reach Heaven, we will have our potentials fully realized. . . . On earth we use only a small part of our potential, but in Heaven we will have our God-given talents released."[10] How does this fuel your anticipation of heaven?

11. Paul Billheimer expands this and sums it all up with the following perspective in his book *Destined for the Throne:*

The Church, then . . . turns out to be the central object, the goal, not only of mundane history but of all that God has been doing in all realms, from all eternity. . . .

From this it is implicit that a godly "romance" is at the heart of the universe and is the key to all existence. . . . John further revealed that this Eternal Companion in God's eternal purpose is to share the Bridegroom's throne following the Marriage Supper of the Lamb (Revelation 3:21). Here we see the ultimate purpose, the climactic goal of history. . . .

Thus the church, and only the church, is the key to and explanation of history. . . . Creation has no other aim. History has no other goal. From before the foundation of the world until the dawn of eternal ages God has been working toward one grand event, one supreme end—the glorious wedding of His Son, the Marriage Supper of the Lamb. . . .

Therefore, from all eternity, all that precedes the Marriage Supper of the Lamb is preliminary and preparatory. Only thereafter will God's program for the eternal ages begin to unfold. God will not be ready, so to speak, to enter upon His ultimate and supreme enterprise for the ages until the Bride is on the throne with her divine Lover and Lord.[11]

Write your responses to the above overview in one-word exclamations:

12. Joni goes on to say: "Is it selfish to run hard in order to gain the prize? Is working toward rewards mercenary? Certainly not. Heavenly crowns are not just rewards for a job well done on earth; when your focus is on Jesus, they are the glorious fulfillment of the job itself."[12]

   a.   Beyond all this, though, she states:

      The Day of Christ would be just that . . . the Day of Christ, not the day of Joni. Glorified hands and feet, as well as reunions with loved ones, began to look more like fringe benefits to the honor of simply being on the invitation list to the coronation party.
      You'll agree. The privilege of casting your crowns at the feet of Jesus will be enough of an honor. Ruling the earth and reigning over angels, becoming pillars within God's

temple and co-heirs of heaven and earth are almost inci-
dental. What we become, receive, and do in heaven won't
be the highlight of heaven. To be there and to *be to the
praise of His glory* will be enough.

It will be Jesus' Day.[13]

    b.   What are your responses to Joni's reflections? What do you
personally look forward to in heaven?

13.   That our heart will be for *Him* and not for our rewards or position is illustrated in Revelation 4:9-11 and 5:8-14. What will all of
heaven (including us) be doing?

    a.   Charles Spurgeon reflects on this as he comments from Song
of Songs, "[The] first word '*Come*' indicates that heaven is a
state of communion. Then it is, '*Come, ye blessed,*' which is a
clear declaration that this is a state of happiness. They cannot be more blessed than they are: they have their hearts'
desire."[14]

    b.   What does David proclaim in Psalm 17:15?

    c.   Express your love to Him now.

Personal Application and Response

14.   Do you just want to say "Wow!" to your discoveries above? What
especially thrills your heart from all you have explored?

    a.   What new *perspective* of this life do the truths of what is
ahead give you?

    b.   What *questions,* if any, does this lesson raise for you?

c. How do your discoveries *motivate* you in your race now?

d. In light of these truths, what *differences*, if any, would you now like to make in how you are currently running? How will you do so? Be specific.

15. Not only do we have a final finish line, but each heat of our race has its own preliminary finish line.

a. What are we told about our times of trial in Psalm 30:4-5, 11-12? How is this endorsed in 1 Peter 5:10-11?

b. Since there is an end to each trial, when we cross the finish line for that season we are rewarded at that time as well. In what similar ways are we rewarded now, as you reflect on our final rewards?

16. Regarding crossing the finish line in our present heat of the race, Michael Yaconelli in his book *Dangerous Wonder* tells of observing a race he'll never forget. It was the girls' 3,200-meter run (eight laps around the track) at the Northern California State Finals for high school track and field. He noticed a girl who was limping badly. He writes:

> When I looked closer, I saw that her legs seemed to be twisted and her feet were turned in at an awkward angle. . . . The bell rang indicating it was time for the contestants to line up. She was not a manager; she stood with the rest of the girls.
> When the gun went off she began racing. . . . After the first lap she was a quarter of a lap behind, and by the time everyone else had finished, she still had one lap to go all by herself. As she went down the backstretch, I could see the agony in her face. Every step she took was excruciat-

ingly painful, but she would not stop. Without realizing it, all of us in the stands had risen to our feet. We were all cheering her on. As she passed by the front of the stands, the noise was overpowering. We were all screaming in unison, "Go! Go! Go!" When she finally crossed the finish line, the crowd erupted in a lengthy ovation.[16]

a. What present difficulties, or even positive challenges, are you experiencing?

b. Can you hear those cheering you on—those who have gone on before as well as those friends who surround you now? Can you hear them yelling for you, "Go! Go! Go!"? Can you hear your Coach cheering? How does this impact you?

c. Most importantly, what perspective are we exhorted to keep in the midst of our trials? See 2 Corinthians 4:13-18. How does this help you persevere in any present difficulty?

17. In *The Sacred Romance*, the authors whet our senses for all that awaits us:

When Paul says, "No eye has seen, no ear has heard, no mind has conceived what God has prepared for those who love him" (1 Cor. 2:9), he simply means we cannot outdream God. What is at the end of our personal journeys? Something beyond our wildest imagination. . . .

Our longing for intimacy gives us the greatest scent of the joys that lie ahead. . . .

When we walk into the crowded excitement of the wedding feast of the Lamb . . . we'll be welcomed to the table by our Lover himself. No one will have to scramble to find another chair, to make room for us. . . . There will be a seat with our name on it, held open at Jesus' command for us and no other.

Heaven is the beginning of an adventure in intimacy. . . . The Holy Spirit, through the human authors of Scripture, chose the imagery of a wedding feast for a reason. . . . What sets this special feast apart from all others is the unique intimacy of the wedding night. The Spirit uses the most secret and tender experience on earth—the union of husband and wife—to convey the depth of intimacy that we will partake with our Lord in heaven.[17]

Stop and savor this reality. Know that this is Christ's invitation to *you!* What is your response? Express your heart to Him now.

18. In concluding this study, these are the words Paul wrote at the conclusion of his life, as rendered in *The Message.* After reading, express your heart to the Lord.

You take over. I'm about to die, my life an offering on God's altar. *This is the only race worth running.* I've run hard right to the finish, believed all the way. All that's left now is the shouting—God's applause. Depend on it, he's an honest judge. He'll do right not only by me, but by everyone eager for his coming[18] (2 Tim. 4:6-8, emphasis mine).

✑ Group Discussion Questions

1. How has this lesson changed your view of heaven and of death?

2. What differences will the truths of this lesson make on how you view your life and your present circumstances? Be specific.

3. How has the imagery of a race throughout this study influenced your perspective of life and your walk with the Lord? How does seeing the end motivate you to grow closer to the Lord now? What changes, if any, will you make in your days or in this season of your life?

4. What values have you discovered through these lessons regarding the key of fixing your eyes on Jesus? How are you now doing this? How has keeping your eyes on Him helped you? Be specific.

5. Spend time worshiping the Lord—thanking, loving, adoring, and glorifying Him.

❧ENDNOTES❧

Chapter 1
1. Henri J. M. Nouwen, *Life of the Beloved* (New York: Crossroad Publishing, 1992), pp. 49, 30-31.
2. Eugene H. Peterson, *Run with the Horses* (Downers Grove, Ill.: InterVarsity, 1983), pp. 38-39.
3. Linda Dillow, *Calm My Anxious Heart* (Colorado Springs: NavPress, 1998), pp. 40-41.
4. Ken Gire, *Windows of the Soul: Experiencing God in New Ways* (Grand Rapids, Mich.: Zondervan, 1996), p. 48.

Chapter 2
1. Brother Lawrence and Frank Laubach, *Practicing His Presence* (Sargent, Ga.: The Seed Sowers, 1973), p. 5.
2. *Devotional Classics*, ed. Richard J. Foster and James Bryan Smith (San Francisco: HarperSanFrancisco, 1993), p. 264.
3. *The Collected Works of Watchman Nee* (Living Streams Ministry, 1993) vol. 38, p. 370.
4. Sheila Walsh, *Honestly* (Grand Rapids: Zondervan, 1996), p. 117.

Chapter 3
1. Elizabeth O'Connor, *Eighth Day of Creation* (Waco, Tex.: Word, 1971), pp. 23, 8.
2. O'Connor, *Eighth Day of Creation*, pp. 40, 24.

Chapter 4
1. Elisabeth Elliot, *Through Gates of Splendor* (New York: Harper & Brothers Publishers, 1957), p. 172.
2. Brent Curtis and John Eldredge, *The Sacred Romance* (Nashville: Nelson, 1997), p. 197.
3. J. Oswald Sanders, *Enjoying Intimacy with God* (Chicago: Moody Press, 1980), pp. 125-26.
4. Oswald Chambers, *My Utmost for His Highest*, updated ed. (Grand Rapids: Discovery House, 1992), September 20.
5. Andrew Murray, *The Believer's Secret of Holiness* (Minneapolis: Bethany House, 1984), pp. 14-15.
6. Chambers, *My Utmost for His Highest*, May 22.
7. Ibid., September 28.
8. Ibid., December 2.
9. Calvin Miller, *Walking with Saints*, (Nashville: Nelson, 1995) pp. 137, 140, 107.
10. Amy Carmichael, *Rose from Brier* (Fort Washington, PA.: Christian Literature Crusade, 1973), p. 87.
11. *The Best of A. W. Tozer*, comp. Warren W. Wiersbe (1978; reprint, Camp Hill, Pa.: Christian Publications, 1995), p. 179.
12. Miller, *Walking with Saints*, pp. 148, 147-48.
13. Curtis and Eldrege, *The Sacred Romance*, pp. 148, 196.

Chapter 5
1. Dr. Jack Daniels, *Daniel's Running Formula*, p. 234.
2. Bill Phillips and Michael D'Orso, *Body for Life* (New York: HarperCollins, 1999), p. xiii.
3. Jerry Brides, *Transforming Grace* (Colorado Springs: NavPress, 1991), pp. 38-39.
4. Walsh, *Honestly*, p. 211.
5. Marsha J. Stevens, "For Those Tears I Died."

Chapter 6
1. Phillips and D'Orso, *Body for Life* , p. 55.
2. Chambers, *My Utmost for His Highest*, January 8.
3. Phillips and D'Orso, *Body for Life*, p. 21.
4. Walsh, *Honestly*, p. 135.

Chapter 7
1. Bridges, *Transforming Grace*, p. 127.
2. Phillips and D'Orso, *Body for Life*, p. 81.
3. Darien B. Cooper, *The Beauty of Beholding God* (Wheaton, Ill.: SP Publications, Victor Books, 1982), p. 53.
4. Richard J. Foster, *Celebration of Discipline* (San Francisco: Harper & Row, 1978), p. 6.
5. Ibid., p. 30.
6. Richard J. Foster, *Prayer* (San Francisco: HarperSanFrancisco, 1992), p. 57.
7. Oswald Chambers, *Daily Thoughts for Disciples* (Grand Rapids: Discovery House, 1994), October 27.
8. Foster, *Prayer*, p. 120.
9. Foster, *Celebration of Discipline*, pp. 31-32.
10. Chambers, *My Utmost for His Highest,* September 10.
11. J. Oswald Sanders, *Enjoying Intimacy with God* (Chicago: Moody, 1980), pp. 11-12, 105.
12. Brother Lawrence and Frank Laubach, *Practicing His Presence* (Sargent, Ga.: The Seed Sowers, 1973), pp. 25-26, 42.
13. Foster, *Prayer*, pp. 47, 49, 52-55.
14. Hannah W. Smith, *God Is Enough* (Grand Rapids: Zondervan, Francis Asbury Press, 1986), p. 78.
15. As quoted by Foster in *Prayer,* p. 47.
16. Miller, *Walking with Saints*, pp. 234-35.
17. Ibid., p. 49.
18. *The Best of A. W. Tozer*, comp. Warren W. Wiersbe (1978; reprint, Camp Hill, Pa.: Christian Publications, 1995), p. 180.
19. Miller, *Walking with Saints*, pp. 50-51.

Chapter 8
1. Watchman Nee, *Christ the Sum of All Spiritual Things* (New York: Christian Fellowship Publishers, 1973), p. 63.
2. V. Raymond Edman, *They Found the Secret* (Grand Rapids: Zondervan, 1984), pp. 137, 139.
3. Watchman Nee, *Sit, Walk, Stand* (Wheaton, Ill.: Tyndale; Fort Washington, Pa.: Christian Literature Crusade, 1977), p. 69.
4. Carole C. Carlson, *Corrie ten Boom: Her Life, Her Faith* (Old Tappan, N.J.: Revell, 1983), p. 116.
5. Madame Jeanne Guyon, *Spiritual Torrents* (Auburn, Maine: The Seed Sowers, 1990), p. 77.
6. Hannah Hurnard, *Hinds' Feet on High Places* (Wheaton, Ill.: Tyndale, 1977), pp. 120-21.

Chapter 9
1. Amy Carmichael, *Rose from Brier* (Fort Washington, Pa.: Christian Literature Crusade, 1973), pp. 78-79.
2. Charles H. Spurgeon, *Morning and Evening* (Grand Rapids: Zondervan, 1980), September 3.
3. Sheila Walsh, *Life Is Tough but God Is Faithful* (Nashville: Thomas Nelson, 1999), p. 20.
4. Chambers, *My Utmost for His Highest*, July 6.
5. Jerry Bridges, *Trusting God* (Colorado Springs: NavPress, 1988), pp. 120-21.
6. Chambers, *My Utmost for His Highest*, September 28.
7. Oswald Chambers, *God's Workmanship* (Grand Rapids: Discovery House, 1997), p. 166.
8. Philip Yancey, *Disappointment with God* (Grand Rapids: Zondervan, 1988), p. 170.
9. Watchman Nee, *The Normal Christian Life* (Wheaton, Ill.: Tyndale; Fort Washington, Pa.: Christian Literature Crusade, 1977), pp. 264-65.

Chapter 10
1. Eugene H. Peterson, *The Message: The New Testament in Contemporary English* (Colorado Springs: NavPress, 1993), p. 474.
2. Sheila Walsh, *Life Is Tough but God Is Faithful* (Nashville: Nelson, 1999), p. 5.
3. Curtis and Eldredge, *The Sacred Romance,* pp. 205, 209.
4. Peterson, *Run with the Horses*, pp. 114, 116-18.
5. Henry Shires, "One Step at a Time," *World Traveler Magazine*, January 2000, p. 58.
6. Ibid.
7. Walsh, *Honestly*, p. 62.
8. John Newton, "Amazing Grace."
9. Anne Graham Lotz, *Just Give Me Jesus* (Nashville: Word, 2000), pp. 168-69.

Chapter 11
1. Gail MacDonald, *High Call, High Privilege* (Peabody, Mass.: Hendrickson Pubishers, Inc. 1998), pp. 50-51.
2. *The Best of A. W. Tozer*, comp. Wiersbe, pp. 8-9.
3. Theodore Monod, *Looking unto Jesus* (Lincoln, Neb.: Back to the Bible, 1991), p. 7.
4. Watchman Nee, *Song of Songs* (Fort Washington, Pa.: Christian Literature Crusade, 1965), p. 33.

Chapter 12
1. J. Oswald Sanders, *Heaven: Better by Far*, rev. ed. (Grand Rapids: Discovery House, 1994), p. 149.
2. Billy Graham, *Hope for the Troubled Heart* (Minneapolis: Grason, 1991), p. 209.
3. *The Best of A. W. Tozer*, comp. Wiersbe, p. 236.
4. Graham, *Hope for the Troubled Heart*, p. 209.
5. Joni Eareckson Tada, *Heaven: Your Real Home* (Grand Rapids: Zondervan, 1995), p. 11.
6. Ibid., p. 51.
7. Ibid., pp. 66-67.
8. Ibid., p. 67.
9. Charles Spurgeon, *The Second Coming of Christ* (New Kensington, Pa.: Whitaker House, 1996), p. 186.
10. Graham, *Hope for the Troubled Heart*, p. 223.
11. Paul E. Billheimer, *Destined for the Throne* (Minneapolis: Bethany House, 1975), pp. 22-23, 26-27.
12. Tada, *Heaven*, p. 90.
13. Ibid., p. 155.
14. Spurgeon, *The Second Coming of Christ*, p. 45.
15. Michael Yaconelli, *Dangerous Wonder* (Colorado Springs: NavPress, 1998), pp. 129-30.
16. Curtis and Eldredge, *The Sacred Romance*, pp. 181-83.
17. Peterson, *The Message*, p. 449.

A Personal Note From the Author

Heart

Jesus Christ is the love of my life! He gives my life purpose and meaning. In running the race I am called to in Him, I have truly found Christ to be the gold. As I've pursued Him through many challenges and adversities, I have found that He is worth it all. Gaining Christ, savoring His love, growing in oneness with Him, and being His instrument in furthering His purposes are joys beyond measure or expression. As I keep my eyes fixed on Him, I want to throw off everything that hinders and run with abandon this race marked out for me. It is my heart to know Him in His fullness, and I encourage you to do so as well—for the fullness of your joy, and for His delight and glory.

Soul

The passage of Scripture upon which this study is based is Hebrews 12:1-3. This exhortation provides direction, motivation, and encouragement for us in our journeys of faith: *Therefore, since we are surrounded by such a great cloud of witnesses, let us throw off everything that hinders and the sin that so easily enables, and let us run with perseverance the race marked out for us. Let us fix our eyes on Jesus, the author and perfecter of our faith, who for the joy set before him endured the cross, scorning its shame, and sat down at the right hand of the throne of God. Consider him who endured such opposition from sinful men, so that you will not grow weary and lose heart.*

Mind

For encouragement in our race from those who have run before us, I recommend to you my study *A Great Cloud of Witnesses*. Exploring how other women have faced challenges in their lives helps us in our circumstances today. Also, as we are exhorted to keep our eyes fixed on Jesus, my study *At Jesus Feet* facilitates our doing so. In addition, for further guidance on how to effectively run our race, I recommend *The Responsive Heart,* my study based on Jesus' parable of the sower.

Strength

Often the difficulties of life can threaten to sideline us in our Christian faith. This study deals with those realities and gives specific guidance in how to overcome them and persevere through hem. I have experienced many difficult trials in my life's journey and have found Christ to be faithful. Even in the darkness, Christ assures us He is with us, sustaining us by His grace, power, strength, and love. How critical it is, I have found, to keep our eyes fixed on Him. As we stay close to Him and draw on His resources, Jesus Christ meets our needs, strengthens us, renews us, and fills us with His very life.

Dear Lord Jesus,
Impart to this one who is precious to You Your vision of who You created her to be and the specific race to which You have called her. Reveal Yourself to her, inspire her to run toward You in heartfelt abandonment. Meet her in Your love, and fill her with Your Spirit. Keep her eyes fixed on You, and enable her to run with perseverance the race marked out for her. Bless her, dear Lord, with Your presence, grace, and love, for her joy and Your glory.
In Jesus' blessed name I pray, Amen.